P9-DUE-504

ESSENTIAL MUIR

Edited with an Introduction by
FRED D. WHITE

Heyday, Berkeley, California

Originally published in conjunction with Santa Clara University as part of the California Legacy series.

Introduction © 2006 by Fred D. White

All rights reserved. No portion of this work may be reproduced or transmitted in any form or by any means, electronic or mechanical, including photocopying and recording, or by any information storage or retrieval system, without permission in writing from Heyday.

Library of Congress Cataloging-in-Publication Data
Muir, John, 1838-1914.
  [Selections. 2006]
  Essential Muir / edited with an introduction by Fred D. White.
      p. cm. -- (A California legacy book)
  Includes bibliographical references.
  ISBN 1-59714-027-9 (pbk. : alk. paper)
  1. Muir, John, 1838-1914. 2. Natural history—United States. 3. Naturalists—United States—Biography. 4. Conservationists—United States—Biography. I. White, Fred D., 1943- II. Title. III. Series.
  QH31.M9A3 2006
  508.7—dc22
                                              2006002511

ISBN: 978-1-59714-027-0

Cover Design: Rebecca LeGates
Interior Design: Philip Krayna, PKD, Berkeley
Typesetting: Lorraine Rath
Printed in Saline, MI, by McNaughton and Gunn

Published by Heyday
P.O. Box 9145, Berkeley, California 94709
(510) 549-3564
heydaybooks.com

20 19 18 17 16

FSC
www.fsc.org
MIX
Paper from
responsible sources
FSC® C011935

ESSENTIAL MUIR

Muir

WITHDRAWN

To Terry Beers and Malcolm Margolin,
for believing I could do this

To my wife, Therese, for her inspiration

And to the spirit of John Muir. May his
voice always be heard...and heeded

Contents

Introduction

Choosing the "essential" works from the catalog of a major author might just be a classic exercise in futility, or at least a classic impertinence, were it not for the likelihood that such winnowing can serve an important educational function. In the case of John Muir (1838–1914), selecting these essential writings is a means of reassessing the importance of an author whose reputation is not quite where it should be. He has been characterized (and caricatured) as a half-cracked hobo who waxed ecstatic in thunderstorms and earthquakes; who foolishly risked his life to experience a glacier or a waterfall up close; who preferred the society of squirrels and trees to people. He has been labeled a Transcendentalist mystic who over-rhapsodized the sublime beauty of wilderness, confusing the boundary between the natural and the supernatural. He has been considered a crotchety activist who would have deprived a major city (San Francisco) of water rather than impede the flow of the Tuolumne River through an uninhabited region (the Hetch Hetchy Valley, just north of the Yosemite Valley). But Muir's legacy is too complex and important to be diminished by caricature and oversimplification.

Muir once described himself as a "poetico-trampo-geologist-botanist and ornithologist-naturalist." It sounds whimsical, yes, but it nicely reflects his desire to fuse rational and investigative sensibilities with aesthetic and spiritual ideas—to be both naturalist *and* nature celebrant. Why should scientific scrutiny of natural phenomena not be in harmony with worshiping nature's beauty, mystery, and power? Like Thoreau, Muir shrugged off the trappings of materialistic living and pursued his own experiment in living simply and purposefully.

Everywhere he looked, nature revealed its glory. (In fact, "glorious" was Muir's favorite word—used to excess, many would agree, but the word best captured his exalted feelings about the wild.) Like the Bible, nature conveyed to him sacred revelations, as when he climbed a giant yellow Ponderosa pine in the Yosemite Valley:

> Climbing these grand trees, especially when they are waving and singing in worship in wind storms, is a glorious experience. Ascending from the lowest branch to the topmost is like stepping up stairs through a blaze of white light, every needle thrilling and shining as if with religious ecstasy.[1]

Muir *ascending*—whether trees, mountains, or glaciers—is Muir in his essence: a man who rejected established religious paths to Heaven, such as the one traveled by his father (who followed the Disciples of Christ[2]), and chose instead to ascend to Heaven via wild nature's path. In choosing this new path to salvation, Muir was not rejecting his Christian faith but extending it, much the way Emerson extended his Christian faith by stepping down as a Unitarian minister and preaching, through poetry and essays, his Transcendentalist credo of finding one's own path to God. As Emerson asserted in his famous (and at the time, notorious) address to the graduating Harvard divinity students in 1837:

> Let me admonish you...to go alone; to refuse the good models, even those which are sacred in the imagination of men, and dare to love God without mediator or veil...Yourself a new-born bard of the Holy Ghost, cast behind you all conformity, and acquaint men at first hand with Deity.

At a meeting of the American Academy of Arts and Letters in New York in January 1916, Robert Underwood Johnson, an editor and longtime friend of Muir, described Muir's religious beliefs this way:

> The love of nature was his religion, but it was not without a personal God, whom he thought as great in the decoration of a

flower as in the launching of a glacier. The old Scotch training
persisted through all his studies of causation, and the keynote
of his philosophy was intelligent and benevolent design..'

Muir's view of nature as infused with spirit, as the very analog
of heaven, is apparent throughout his oeuvre. The tree-climbing
passage above is one example; here is another, straight from one of
his earliest Yosemite journals. Moved by the power of a waterfall,
he records the sublime moment of transport:

> One stupendous unit of light and song, perfect and harmoni-
> ous as any in heaven…If my soul could get away from this
> so-called prison, be granted all the list of attributes generally
> bestowed on spirits, my first ramble on spirit wings…I should
> study nature's laws.'

It is tempting to regard Muir's wilderness quest as religious.
However, it may have been, initially, a reaction to his father's
unyielding orthodoxy, which included intolerance for intellectual
curiosity. Any derelictions of duty brought down the whip. Daniel
Muir put his son to the plow at age twelve, forcing him to work
sixteen hours a day, six days a week, even when John was ill with
the mumps and unable to swallow anything except milk. Only
when he contracted pneumonia, as Muir explains in his autobiography, *The Story of My Boyhood and Youth,* was he allowed to remain in
bed; but no doctor was called in, "for father…believed that God and
hard work were by far the best doctors." Muir's assessment of that
credo was blunt: "We were all made slaves through the vice of over-
industry." It wasn't just "over-industry" but deprivation of liberty
as well. Perhaps in his ecstatic responses to finding himself in the
wild—he often leaped about, singing, with open arms—Muir was
demonstrating, if only to himself, that for the soul to flourish it
must break free of all restraint. His siblings, he realized, experienced
a similar craving for freedom. When his artist-sister Mary wrote to
him in distress after their father had flung her drawings into the
mud "to save her soul," Muir promptly sent her enough money to
leave home.

What must have been most hurtful to Muir was Daniel's contempt for his son's wilderness explorations. After reading his son's

account of a snowstorm atop Mt. Shasta in 1874, Daniel wrote the following to him:

> I knew it was not God's work [you were doing], although you seem to think you are doing God's service. If it had not been for God's boundless mercy you would have been cut off in the midst of your folly…know that the world and the church of the world will glory in such as you, but how can they believe which receive honor of one another and seek not the honor that cometh from God only [;] John 5,44. You cannot warm the heart of the saint of God with your cold icy-topped mountains.[5]

Daniel concludes the letter by saying it would be better that John burn his book rather than continue working on it and publishing it, "and then it will do no more harm either to you or to others."

Muir's genius as a nature writer has forged in the public mind the majesty of Sierra and Alaskan wilderness. The mere mention of his name conjures up those majestic emblems of Yosemite—Half Dome, El Capitan, the giant sequoias, bald eagles—which in turn conjure up the idea of California itself, as the California state quarter, minted in 2005, attests. However, these associations alone cannot do justice to the polymath and autodidact whose genius also had a technical, mechanical, and rigorously scientific side as well. Long before he began writing, Muir loved inventing—machines that were as practical as they were fanciful. He avidly studied botany and the embryonic sciences of geology and glaciology. And we should not overlook the fact that Muir was, from his earliest years, a humanist and a person of compassion—a compassion that extended to animals. In fact, some of his most poignant childhood memories involved animals, such as Nob, "the most faithful, intelligent, playful, affectionate, human-like horse I ever knew," who died of pneumonia. He even loved the little black water bugs that congregated on their farm's Fountain Lake. "Their whole lives seemed to be play," he writes in his autobiography, "skimming, swimming, swirling, and waltzing together in little groups." The moral lesson here is that animals are to be respected as kindred spirits: "Thus godlike sympathy grows and thrives and spreads far beyond the teachings of churches and schools, where too often the mean, blinding, loveless doctrine is taught that animals have neither mind nor soul, have no rights that we are bound to respect."

But it is as a literary artist, manifest in all of his works, that John Muir reaches us most powerfully today.

Muir's Literary Legacy

Not much is known about Muir's sense of his own literary artistry. We do know that he resisted what he referred to disdainfully as "bookmaking." The disdain comes largely from his favoring first-hand experience in the world over vicarious experience derived from books. As he wrote in his journal around 1872, "No amount of word-making will ever make a single soul to know these mountains...One day's exposure to mountains is better than cartloads of books."

The only writing he truly enjoyed was journal writing—field notes and drawings. Writing for publication, however, required confining himself indoors (he dubbed the study in his Martinez home his "scribble den"); it required transmuting his fragmentary, spontaneously generated journal entries into fully developed, coherent discourse. For Muir this was devilishly hard work. Explains Marion Randall Parsons, who boarded Muir when he was working on *Travels in Alaska,* "Composition was always slow and laborious for him...Each sentence, each phrase, each word underwent his critical scrutiny, not once but twenty times before he was satisfied to let it stand."⁶

But his resistance to writing books is not as paradoxical as it seems. Muir wrote as naturally as he walked and rejoiced in nature—but it was spontaneous writing. His journal was part of his amazingly sparse backpack, accompanied by three books (the New Testament, *Paradise Lost,* and Robert Burns's poems), a change of clothes, bread, and tea. He wrote his journals and sketched with pencils; sometimes when he wrote letters, he made his own ink out of tree sap. By limiting himself to these bare essentials, thereby simplifying his life in true Thoreauvian fashion, his life fell into harmony with the wilderness—and he wanted his writing to capture that simplicity and harmony. Muir's writing, we might say, was a kind of spontaneously generated singing from the soul. Writing was as essential a life-function as walking, seeing, breathing.

For someone who did not regard himself as "a writer," Muir possessed a profoundly poetic sensibility. He recognized this sensibility himself early on, and wondered if he could manifest it by literally writing poetry—but no; the few poems of Muir's that survive make it clear that his poetic soul would not manifest itself in traditional verse.

Page randomly through Muir's writings, and the first thing you will probably notice is the way he shifts almost seamlessly from the rhapsodic to the scientific and back again. In virtually one breath, Muir can rejoice in the celestial power of a Yosemite waterfall and describe plant species with botanical precision. He can be expressive as a giddy child in one paragraph and professorial in the next. Was this symptomatic of a schizophrenic sensibility? No. Muir strove in his writing, as he did in his life, to fuse the two sensibilities together. If Muir is not as widely read today as he should be, it is probably because his works are neither "scientific" nor "literary" in the traditional sense of those terms, but a fusion of both.

The most dramatic achievement resulting from this fusion of sensibilities occurred when Muir demonstrated beyond a reasonable doubt the glacial origin of the Yosemite Valley. Not only did he collect geological evidence of, for example, glacial striae (scrapings on rock faces that could only have been caused by glacial movement), but he quite transcended conventional scientific procedure altogether by *living like a glacier.* As he explained in an 1871 letter to his lifelong friend and mentor, the educator and botanist Mrs. Jeanne Carr:

> I can do much of this ice work in the quiet, and the whole subject is purely physical, so that I can get but little from books. All depends upon the goodness of one's eyes. No scientific book in the world can tell me how this Yosemite granite is put together, or how it has been taken down. Patient observation and constant brooding above the rocks, lying upon them for years as the ice did, is the way to arrive at the truths which are graven so lavishly upon them.

How This Book Is Organized

Refreshingly, Muir defies labeling, and so, in surveying his considerable body of work, one does not find mutually exclusive categories; instead, we can identify phases in which we see one of five sensibilities manifested. Accordingly, I have organized the selections in the context of these sensibilities, which I call, in chronological order, The Visionary Inventor, The Wandering Minstrel, The Nature Scribe and Rhapsode, The Global Adventurer, and The Planet Steward.

The Visionary Inventor

Because his father forbade him to read novels ("The Deevil's ain buik o' lies!" was Daniel Muir's assessment of a novel.'), John would get up in the middle of the night to read on the sly, but during the winter months, when a fire was needed, his father would awaken. And so John shifted his attention to an equally joyous pursuit, inventing fanciful yet practical machines such as a plant-growth measurer, an all-in-one barometer/hygrometer/pyrometer, a study desk that automatically rotated his books, and various early-rising machines, including a bed that propped the sleeper upright on the floor at the pre-appointed time. In *The Story of My Boyhood and Youth* (1913), Muir captures the delight of such inventiveness, which proved to be an antidote to the drudgery of farm life and his father's relentlessly harsh rule.

The Wandering Minstrel

Muir's first major excursion into wilderness took place during the Civil War. A committed pacifist, he ventured into the woodlands and marshes of northern Michigan and then crossed the border into Canada, where he remained until 1866, working as a machinist and teaching. Back in the U.S., he went to work for a wagon parts manufacturer in Indianapolis. One evening in March 1867, while adjusting a machine belt, he lost his grip on a file, which flew into his right eye, causing temporary blindness in both eyes. The terror, however short-lived, of losing his sight forever motivated him to reassess his priorities, and later that year he boarded a train for

Louisville, Kentucky, to fulfill his dream of exploring the wilderness areas of the South. From Louisville he set out on a two-month, thousand-mile walk through Kentucky, Tennessee (via the Cumberland Mountains—"the first real mountains that my foot ever touched or eyes beheld"), across the western tip of North Carolina, then diagonally across Northern Georgia, down the Savannah River to the Atlantic, where he boarded a steamship to Florida. He then traveled across Florida to Cedar Keys on the Gulf Coast. He'd originally planned to sail to South America, but had fallen ill with malaria. After recuperating in Havana, he set sail to San Francisco.

Although the resulting book, *A Thousand Mile Walk to the Gulf*, published posthumously in 1916, is composed of reworked journal entries (characteristic of most of Muir's books), it retains much of the spontaneity of the original entries. These writings capture well their author's wanderlust heart, but they also capture, as one of his biographers, Herbert F. Smith so aptly states, "the narrative of a man who had not yet made up his mind" about the direction his life was to take.[8]

THE NATURE SCRIBE AND RHAPSODE

With the wilderness now in his blood, and having read about the sublime, vast mountain wildernesses of the Sierra—especially of the Yosemite Valley—Muir was eager to embark on the path that would enable him to bring his gifts as a naturalist to fruition. Like the great geologist Louis Agassiz, who had first theorized the existence of an Ice Age and of glaciation, Muir believed that "a physical fact is as sacred as a moral principle."[9]

On virtually every page of his Sierra books—*The Mountains of California* (1894), *My First Summer in the Sierra* (1911), and *The Yosemite* (1912)—we feel the author's awe at the majesty of mountain wilderness, enhanced rather than diminished by his well-trained scientific scrutiny, as in this description of Sierra summit trees from *The Mountains of California*:

> There are two trees in the Sierra forests that are never blown down, so long as they continue in sound health. These are the

juniper and the dwarf pine of the summit peaks. Their stiff, crooked roots grip the storm-beaten ledges like eagles' claws, while their lithe, cord-like branches bend round compliantly, offering but slight holds for winds, however violent. The other alpine conifers—the needle pine, mountain pine, two-leaved pine, and hemlock spruce—are never thinned out by this agent to any destructive extent, on account of their growth.

Even Muir's letters often possess the same fusion of reportage and poetic description, as in the two letters to Jeanne Carr that appear in this section. Jeanne Carr, wife of the botanist and Berkeley professor Ezra Carr (with whom Muir had studied when they were both at the University of Wisconsin in the early 1860s), nurtured Muir's botanical and geological studies in the wild and encouraged—prodded—him to publish. "She formed the bridge between the crabbed isolation of his boyhood and the world of men he would have to live in," writes Linnie Marsh Wolfe in her biography of Muir. "By her unfailing tact and faith in his genius, she directed his aims and helped fit him for leadership." I venture to add that she was also his muse, inspiring him, as in his "Nut Time" letter, to such eloquent flights of fancy as to make him seem like a jubilant Tom O' Bedlam.

THE GLOBAL ADVENTURER

John Muir the adventurer was not too different from John Muir the wanderer, or the poet-naturalist, or even the inventor-machinist. The distinctions are matters of degree, or of principal sensibility. For example, while in Yosemite, he put his machinist's skills to use in helping to operate a sawmill. He was certainly the adventurer when he rode a snow avalanche down the north slope of Cloud's Rest in Yosemite, or when he perched himself on a lip of rock in order to better experience the sensation of a waterfall—adventures he relates in *The Yosemite,* Chapters 1 and 3, respectively. His sensibilities were different in each "incarnation," however. In Wisconsin his focus was to learn and to create labor-saving devices that would free him to study, or enable him to earn more money; on his thousand-mile trek through the South, it was to experience freedom, to discover himself.

In California it was to exult in the sublime beauty of the Sierra and to solve the mystery of how the Yosemite Valley had formed.

But something else stirred in Muir's blood: a sheer craving for adventure—adventure for its own sake, for the intrinsic life-thrills it provided. It is what his near-contemporary, Jack London, would refer to as "the call of the wild."

And so, in 1879, Muir heeded the calling of the northern wildernesses of Puget Sound, British Columbia, and especially Alaska, which, although it had already begun to be exploited by whites for its resources, was as close to pristine, untamed wilderness as Muir would ever see in North America. During these Alaska trips, Muir also began to pay close attention to the native peoples and their customs (See "Eskimos and Walrus").

Soon after marrying Louisiana ("Louie") Strenzel in 1880 and beginning a happy, successful family life, Muir embarked on his second Alaska adventure—a glacier-exploration trip that resulted in his most popular book. Accompanied by a little black border collie mutt, whom he named Stickeen (after the Stickeen Indians, who had originally adopted him), Muir ventured into Taylor Bay to explore on foot a newly discovered glacier but got trapped. In *Stickeen* (1909), first published in *Overland Monthly* as "An Adventure with a Dog and a Glacier," Muir demonstrates his exceptional storytelling ability. Also, in a mysterious way, the intrepid little dog seems to embody all that Muir himself represented. As Malcolm Margolin explains in his afterword to the illustrated Heyday Books edition of the story, "It was as if the dog—driven to its utmost limits that day on the glacier—became momentarily transparent; and when Muir looked through to the essence of its being, what he saw in Stickeen was not very different from what he saw in himself."

THE PLANET STEWARD

One might argue that anyone who revered the natural world in all of its manifestations, as did John Muir from his earliest romps in the fields of his native Scotland, is well on the way toward becoming an environmentalist. After all, one never has to look very far to find evidence of nature being ravaged. Muir had also long been keenly aware of humanity's role in environmental destruction from having read George Perkins Marsh's *Man and Nature* (1864), a revolutionary and unprecedented investigation of human environmental destruction since ancient times. Marsh asserts:

> Man is everywhere a disturbing agent. Wherever he plants his foot, the harmonies of nature are turned to discords. The proportions and accommodations which ensured the stability of existing arrangements are overthrown. Indigenous vegetable and animal species are extirpated, and supplanted by others of foreign origin, spontaneous production is forbidden or restricted, and the face of the earth is either laid bare or covered with a new and reluctant growth of vegetable forms, and with alien tribes of animal life...The fact that, of all organic beings, man alone is to be regarded as essentially a destructive power...tends to prove that, though living in physical nature, he is not of her.

One cannot help but suspect that Muir, after reading the above passage, felt compelled to prove Marsh right...and wrong: right in Marsh's diagnosis of humanity's destructive legacy, but wrong in his conclusion that human beings are not a part of nature.

In 1876, after sojourning among the giant sequoias and observing their rapid decimation, he published "God's First Temples: How Shall We Preserve Our Forests?" This powerful piece gave the public a vivid overview of forest destruction and advanced the case for federal protection. But it wasn't until 1889 that Muir turned his attention full time to the rapidly developing environmental crises in California. After surveying the destruction in Yosemite with Robert Underwood Johnson (an editor at *Century Magazine*), the two men decided to make the case for federal protection of the area, to advocate making it a national park. Johnson would lobby in Washington, D.C.; Muir would write articles for *Century*. Their plan worked, and in the fall of 1889 Congress passed a bill to make Yosemite a national park, effective the following year. Over the next decade, forest reserves were created. In 1892 Muir and a group of wilderness enthusiasts formed the Sierra Club, and Muir was elected its first president—a position he retained until his death.

John Muir scrutinized and celebrated wild nature on behalf of the human soul. Can he still speak to us today? Yes, but we must learn to take him seriously even though the world is too much with us, as Wordsworth lamented two hundred years ago in a famous sonnet, adding, "Little we see in nature that is ours." Muir can teach us once again to see what is ours in the natural world.

"Go now and then for fresh life," he wrote in his journal on the way to the Yosemite Valley in September 1874, "[Even] if most of humanity must go through this down stage of development—just as divers hold their breath and come ever and anon to the surface to breathe...go to the snow flowers in winter, to the sunflowers in summer...Go up and away for life."[10] He is not merely telling us to jump into our RVs and spend a weekend in the mountains; he is reminding us that, like Antaeus, we cannot remain uprooted from the earth for too long without losing our sense of what it means to be fully alive.

Notes

1. *The Yosemite* (New York: Century, 1912: 66)

2. An evangelical, utopian sect founded in America by the Scotsman Alexander Campbell. Unlike Calvinism, and more in keeping with the spirit of American democracy and liberty, it held that salvation was available to anyone, not just to a pre-ordained "Elect."

3. Robert Underwood Johnson, "John Muir as I Knew Him," in *John Muir: His Life and Letters and Other Writings*, ed. Terry Gifford (London: Baton Wicks, 1996)

4. *John of the Mountains: The Unpublished Journals of John Muir* (Madison: University of Wisconsin Press, 1979); Jan. 18, 1869

5. *Life and Letters of John Muir*, ed. William Frederick Bade (Boston and New York: Houghton Mifflin, 1924), I:20-22

6. Marion Randall Parsons, "John Muir and the Alaska Book," in *John Muir: His Life and Letters and Other Writings*, 884

7. Quoted by Linnie Marsh Wolfe, *Son of the Wilderness: The Life of John Muir* (New York: A. A. Knopf, 1945), 46

8. Herbert F. Smith, *John Muir* (New York: Twayne, 1965), 35

9. Agassiz in conversation with his pupils, with whom he traveled to Lake Superior in 1848; quoted by Linnie Marsh Wolfe in *Son of the Wilderness*

10. *John of the Mountains*, 191

PART ONE:

The Visionary Inventor

Knowledge and Inventions

Several of our neighbors had brought a dozen or two of all sorts of books, which I borrowed and read, keeping all of them except the religious ones carefully hidden from Father's eye. Among these were Scott's novels, which, like all other novels, were strictly forbidden but devoured with glorious pleasure in secret. Father was easily persuaded to buy Josephus' *Wars of the Jews*, and d'Aubigné's *History of the Reformation*, and I tried hard to get him to buy Plutarch's *Lives*, which, as I told him, everybody, even religious people, praised as a grand good book; but he would have nothing to do with the old pagan until the graham bread and anti-flesh doctrines came suddenly into our backwoods neighborhood, making a stir something like phrenology and spirit-rappings, which were as mysterious in their attacks as influenza. He then thought it possible that Plutarch might be turned to account on the food question by revealing what those old Greeks and Romans ate to make them strong; and so at last we gained our glorious Plutarch. Dick's *Christian Philosopher*, which I borrowed from a neighbor, I thought I might venture to read in the open, trusting that the word "Christian" would be proof against its cautious condemnation. But Father balked at the word "philosopher," and quoted from the Bible a verse that spoke of "philosophy falsely so-called." I then ventured to speak in defense of the book, arguing that we could not do without at least a little of the most useful kinds of philosophy.

"Yes, we can," he said with enthusiasm. "The Bible is the only book human beings can possibly require throughout all the journey from earth to heaven."

"But how," I contended, "can we find the way to heaven without the Bible, and how after we grow old can we read the Bible without

a little helpful science? Just think, Father, you cannot read your
Bible without spectacles, and millions of others are in the same
fix; and spectacles cannot be made without some knowledge of the
science of optics."

"Oh!" he replied, perceiving the drift of the argument. "There
will always be plenty of worldly people to make spectacles."

To this I stubbornly replied with a quotation from the Bible
with reference to the time coming when "all shall know the Lord
from the least even to the greatest," and then who will make the
spectacles? But he still objected to my reading that book, called me
a contumacious quibbler too fond of disputation, and ordered me
to return it to the accommodating owner. I managed, however, to
read it later.

On the food question, Father insisted that those who argued for
a vegetable diet were in the right, because our teeth showed plainly
that they were made with reference to fruit and grain and not for
flesh like those of dogs and wolves and tigers. He therefore promptly
adopted a vegetable diet and requested mother to make the bread
from graham flour instead of bolted flour. Mother put both kinds
on the table, and meat also, to let all the family take their choice,
and while Father was insisting on the foolishness of eating flesh, I
came to her help by calling Father's attention to the passage in the
Bible which told the story of Elijah the prophet who, when he was
pursued by enemies who wanted to take his life, was hidden by
the Lord by the brook Cherith, and fed by ravens; and surely the
Lord knew what was good to eat, whether bread or meat. And on
what, I asked, did the Lord feed Elijah? On vegetables or graham
bread? No, he directed the ravens to feed his prophet on flesh. The
Bible being the sole rule, Father at once acknowledged that he was
mistaken. The Lord never would have sent flesh to Elijah by the
ravens if graham bread were better.

I remember as a great and sudden discovery that the poetry
of the Bible, Shakespeare, and Milton was a source of inspiring,
exhilarating, uplifting pleasure; and I became anxious to know all
the poets and saved up small sums to buy as many of their books
as possible. Within three or four years I was the proud possessor of
parts of Shakespeare's, Milton's, Cowper's, Henry Kirke White's,

Campbell's, and Akenside's works, and quite a number of others seldom read nowadays. I think it was in my fifteenth year that I began to relish good literature with enthusiasm, and smack my lips over favorite lines, but there was desperately little time for reading, even in the winter evenings—only a few stolen minutes now and then. Father's strict rule was, straight to bed immediately after family worship, which in winter was usually over by eight o'clock. I was in the habit of lingering in the kitchen with a book and candle after the rest of the family had retired, and considered myself fortunate if I got five minutes' reading before Father noticed the light and ordered me to bed; an order that, of course, I immediately obeyed. But night after night I tried to steal minutes in the same lingering way, and how keenly precious those minutes were, few nowadays can know. Father failed perhaps two or three times in a whole winter to notice my light for nearly ten minutes, magnificent golden blocks of time, long to be remembered like holidays or geological periods. One evening when I was reading Church history, Father was particularly irritable and called out with hope-killing emphasis, "John, go to bed! Must I give you a separate order every night to get you to go to bed? Now, I will have no irregularity in the family; you must go when the rest go, and without my having to tell you." Then, as an afterthought, as if judging that his words and tone of voice were too severe for so pardonable an offense as reading a religious book, he unwarily added: "If you will read, get up in the morning and read. You may get up in the morning as early as you like."

That night I went to bed wishing with all my heart and soul that somebody or something might call me out of sleep to avail myself of this wonderful indulgence, and next morning to my joyful surprise I awoke before Father called me. A boy sleeps soundly after working all day in the snowy woods, but that frosty morning I sprang out of bed as if called by a trumpet blast, rushed downstairs, scarce feeling my chilblains, enormously eager to see how much time I had won; and when I held up my candle to a little clock that stood on a bracket in the kitchen I found that it was only one o'clock. I had gained five hours, almost half a day! "Five hours to myself!" I said, "five huge, solid hours!" I can hardly think of any other event in my life, any

discovery I ever made that gave birth to joy so transportingly glorious as the possession of these five frosty hours.

In the glad, tumultuous excitement of so much suddenly
acquired time-wealth, I hardly knew what to do with it. I first
thought of going on with my reading, but the zero weather would
make a fire necessary, and it occurred to me that Father might
object to the cost of firewood that took time to chop. Therefore, I
prudently decided to go down cellar and begin work on a model of a
self-setting sawmill I had invented. Next morning I managed to get
up at the same gloriously early hour, and though the temperature
of the cellar was a little below the freezing point, and my light was
only a tallow candle, the mill work went joyfully on. There were a
few tools in a corner of the cellar—a vise, files, a hammer, chisels,
etc., that Father had brought from Scotland, but no saw excepting
a coarse, crooked one that was unfit for sawing dry hickory or oak.
So I made a fine-tooth saw suitable for my work out of a strip of
steel that had formed part of an old-fashioned corset, which cut the
hardest wood smoothly. I also made my own bradawls, punches,
and a pair of compasses, out of wire and old files.

My workshop was immediately under Father's bed, and the fil-
ing and tapping in making cogwheels, journals, cams, etc., must, no
doubt, have annoyed him, but with the permission he had granted
in his mind, and doubtless hoping that I would soon tire of getting
up at one o'clock, he impatiently waited about two weeks before
saying a word. I did not vary more than five minutes from one
o'clock all winter, nor did I feel any bad effects whatever, nor did
I think at all about the subject as to whether so little sleep might
be in any way injurious; it was a grand triumph of willpower over
cold and common comfort and work-weariness in abruptly cutting
down my ten hours' allowance of sleep to five. I simply felt that I
was rich beyond anything I could have dreamed of or hoped for.
I was far more than happy. Like Tam O'Shanter I was glorious,
"O'er a' the ills o' life victorious."

Father, as was customary in Scotland, gave thanks and asked a
blessing before meals, not merely as a matter of form and decent
Christian manners, for he regarded food as a gift derived directly
from the hands of the Father in heaven. Therefore, every meal to

him was a sacrament requiring conduct and attitude of mind not unlike that befitting the Lord's Supper. No idle word was allowed to be spoken at our table, much less any laughing or fun or story-telling. When we were at the breakfast table, about two weeks after the great golden time discovery, Father cleared his throat prelimi-nary, as we all knew, to saying something considered important. I feared that it was to be on the subject of my early rising and dreaded the withdrawal of the permission he had granted on account of the noise I made, but still hoped that, as he had given his word that I might get up as early as I wished, he would as a Scotchman stand to it, even though it was given in an unguarded moment and taken in a sense unreasonably far-reaching. The solemn sacramental silence was broken by the dreaded question:

"John, what time is it when you get up in the morning?"

"About one o'clock," I replied in a low, meek, guilty tone of voice.

"And what kind of a time is that, getting up in the middle of the night and disturbing the whole family?"

I simply reminded him of the permission he had freely granted me to get up as early as I wished.

"I know it," he said in an almost agonized tone of voice. "I know I gave you that miserable permission, but I never imagined that you would get up in the middle of the night."

To this I cautiously made no reply, but continued to listen for the heavenly one o'clock call, and it never failed.

After completing my self-setting sawmill I dammed one of the streams in the meadow and put the mill in operation. This inven-tion was speedily followed by a lot of others—waterwheels, curious door locks and latches, thermometers, hygrometers, pyrometers, clocks, a barometer, an automatic contrivance for feeding the horses at any required hour, a lamplighter and fire-lighter, an early- or-late-rising machine, and so forth.

After the sawmill was proved and discharged from my mind, I happened to think it would be a fine thing to make a timekeeper which would tell the day of the week and the day of the month, as well as strike like a common clock and point out the hours; also to have an attachment whereby it could be connected with a bedstead to set me on my feet at any hour in the morning; also to start fires,

light lamps, etc. I had learned the time laws of the pendulum from
a book, but with this exception I knew nothing of timekeepers, for
I had never seen the inside of any sort of clock or watch. After long
brooding, the novel clock was at length completed in my mind, and
was tried and found to be durable and to work well and look well
before I had begun to build it in wood. I carried small parts of it in
my pocket to whittle at when I was out at work on the farm, using
every spare or stolen moment within reach without Father's knowing anything about it. In the middle of summer, when harvesting
was in progress, the novel time machine was nearly completed. It
was hidden upstairs in a spare bedroom where some tools were kept.
I did the making and mending on the farm, but one day at noon,
when I happened to be away, Father went upstairs for a hammer
or something and discovered the mysterious machine back of the
bedstead. My sister Margaret saw him on his knees examining it,
and at the first opportunity whispered in my ear, "John, Father saw
that thing you're making upstairs." None of the family knew what I
was doing, but they knew very well that all such work was frowned
on by Father and kindly warned me of any danger that threatened
my plans. The fine invention seemed doomed to destruction before
its time-ticking commenced, though I thought it handsome, had so
long carried it in my mind, and like the nest of Burns's wee mousie,
it had cost me many a weary whittling nibble. When we were at
dinner several days after the sad discovery, Father began to clear his
throat to speak, and I feared the doom of martyrdom was about to
be pronounced on my grand clock.

"John," he inquired, "what is that thing you are making
upstairs?"

I replied in desperation that I didn't know what to call it.

"What! You mean to say you don't know what you are trying
to do?"

"Oh, yes," I said, "I know very well what I am doing."

"What, then, is the thing for?"

"It's for a lot of things," I replied, "but getting people up early in
the morning is one of the main things it is intended for; therefore,
it might perhaps be called an early-rising machine."

After getting up so extravagantly early all the last memorable
winter, to make a machine for getting up perhaps still earlier

seemed so ridiculous that he very nearly laughed. But after con-
trolling himself and getting command of a sufficiently solemn face
and voice he said severely, "Do you not think it is very wrong to
waste your time on such nonsense?"

"No," I said meekly. "I don't think I'm doing any wrong."

"Well," he replied, "I assure you I do, and if you were only half
as zealous in the study of religion as you are in contriving and
whittling these useless, nonsensical things, it would be infinitely
better for you. I want you to be like Paul, who said that he desired
to know nothing among men but Christ and Him crucified."

To this I made no reply, gloomily believing my fine machine
was to be burned but still taking what comfort I could in realizing
that anyhow I had enjoyed inventing and making it.

After a few days, finding that nothing more was to be said and
that Father after all had not had the heart to destroy it, all necessity
for secrecy being ended, I finished it in the half-hours that we had
at noon and set it in the parlor between two chairs, hung moraine
boulders that had come from the direction of Lake Superior on it
for weights, and set it running. We were then hauling grain into
the barn. Father at this period devoted himself entirely to the Bible
and did no farm work whatever. The clock had a good loud tick,
and when he heard it strike, one of my sisters told me that he left
his study, went to the parlor, got down on his knees and carefully
examined the machinery, which was all in plain sight, not being
enclosed in a case. This he did repeatedly, and evidently seemed
a little proud of my ability to invent and whittle such a thing,
though careful to give no encouragement for anything more of the
kind in future.

The World and the University

When I told Father that I was about to leave home and inquired whether, if I should happen to be in need of money, he would send me a little, he said, "No; depend entirely on yourself." Good advice, I suppose, but surely needlessly severe for a bashful, home-loving boy who had worked so hard. I had the gold sovereign that my grandfather had given me when I left Scotland, and a few dollars, perhaps ten, that I had made by raising a few bushels of grain on a little patch of sandy, abandoned ground. So when I left home to try the world, I had only about fifteen dollars in my pocket.

Strange to say, Father carefully taught us to consider ourselves very poor worms of the dust, conceived in sin, etc., and devoutly believed that quenching every spark of pride and self-confidence was a sacred duty, without realizing that in so doing he might at the same time be quenching everything else. Praise he considered most venomous, and tried to assure me that when I was fairly out in the wicked world making my own way I would soon learn that although I might have thought him a hard taskmaster at times, strangers were far harder. On the contrary, I found no lack of kindness and sympathy. All the baggage I carried was a package made up of the two clocks and a small thermometer made of a piece of old washboard, all three tied together, with no covering or case of any sort, the whole looking like one very complicated machine.

The aching parting from mother and my sisters was, of course, hard to bear. Father let David drive me down to Pardeeville, a place I had never before seen, though it was only nine miles south of the Hickory Hill home. When we arrived at the village tavern, it seemed deserted. Not a single person was in sight. I set my clock baggage on the rickety platform. David said good-bye and started for home, leaving me alone in the world. The grinding noise made by the wagon in turning short brought out the landlord, and the first thing that caught his eye was my strange bundle. Then he looked at me and said, "Hello, young man, what's this?"

"Machines," I said, "for keeping time and getting up in the morning, and so forth."

"Well! Well! That's a mighty queer getup. You must be a down-east Yankee. Where did you get the pattern for such a thing?"

"In my head," I said.

Someone down the street happened to notice the landlord looking intently at something and came up to see what it was. Three or four people in that little village formed an attractive crowd, and in fifteen or twenty minutes the greater part of the population of Pardeeville stood gazing in a circle around my strange hickory belongings. I kept outside of the circle to avoid being seen and had the advantage of hearing the remarks without being embarrassed. Almost everyone as he came up would say, "What's that? What's it for? Who made it?" The landlord would answer them all alike, "Why, a young man that lives out in the country somewhere made it, and he says it's a thing for keeping time, getting up in the morning, and something that I didn't understand. I don't know what he meant." "Oh, no!" one of the crowd would say, "that can't be. It's for something else—something mysterious. Mark my words, you'll see all about it in the newspapers some of these days." A curious little fellow came running up the street, joined the crowd, stood on tiptoe to get sight of the wonder, quickly made up his mind, and shouted in crisp, confident, cock-crowing style, "I know what that contraption's for. It's a machine for taking the bones out of fish."

This was in the time of the great popular phrenology craze, when the fences and barns along the roads throughout the country were plastered with big skull-bump posters, headed, "Know Thyself," and advising everybody to attend schoolhouse lectures to have their heads explained and be told what they were good for and whom they ought to marry. My mechanical bundle seemed to bring a good deal of this phrenology to mind, for many of the onlookers would say, "I wish I could see that boy's head—he must have a tremendous bump of invention." Others complimented me by saying, "I wish I had that fellow's head. I'd rather have it than the best farm in the state."

I stayed overnight at this little tavern, waiting for a train. In the morning I went to the station and set my bundle on the platform. Along came the thundering train, a glorious sight, the first train I had ever waited for. When the conductor saw my queer baggage, he cried, "Hello! What have we here?"

"Inventions for keeping time, early rising, and so forth. May I take them into the car with me?"

"You can take them where you like," he replied, "but you had better give them to the baggage-master. If you take them into the car they will draw a crowd and might get broken."

So I gave them to the baggage-master and made haste to ask the conductor whether I might ride on the engine. He good-naturedly said, "Yes, it's the right place for you. Run ahead, and tell the engineer what I say." But the engineer bluntly refused to let me on, saying, "It don't matter what the conductor told you. I say you can't ride on my engine."

By this time the conductor, standing ready to start his train, was watching to see what luck I had, and when he saw me returning came ahead to meet me.

"The engineer won't let me on," I reported.

"Won't he?" said the kind conductor. "Oh! I guess he will. You come down with me." And so he actually took the time and patience to walk the length of that long train to get me onto the engine.

"Charlie," said he, addressing the engineer, "don't you ever take a passenger?"

"Very seldom," he replied.

"Anyhow, I wish you would take this young man on. He has the strangest machines in the baggage car I ever saw in my life. I believe he could make a locomotive. He wants to see the engine running. Let him on." Then in a low whisper, he told me to jump on, which I did gladly, the engineer offering neither encouragement nor objection.

As soon as the train was started, the engineer asked what the "strange thing" the conductor spoke of really was.

"Only inventions for keeping time, getting folk up in the morning, and so forth," I hastily replied, and before he could ask any more questions I asked permission to go outside of the cab to see the machinery. This he kindly granted, adding, "Be careful not to fall off, and when you hear me whistling for a station you come back, because if it is reported against me to the superintendent that I allow boys to run all over my engine, I might lose my job."

Assuring him that I would come back promptly, I went out and walked along the footboard on the side of the boiler, watching the magnificent machine rushing through the landscapes as if glorying in its strength like a living creature. While seated on the cowcatcher platform, I seemed to be fairly flying, and the wonderful display of power and motion was enchanting. This was the first time I had ever been on a train, much less a locomotive, since I had left Scotland. When I got to Madison, I thanked the kind conductor and engineer for my glorious ride, inquired the way to the Fair, shouldered my inventions, and walked to the fairground.

When I applied for an admission ticket at a window by the gate I told the agent that I had something to exhibit.

"What is it?" he inquired.

"Well, here it is. Look at it."

When he craned his neck through the window and got a glimpse of my bundle, he cried excitedly, "Oh! You don't need a ticket. Come right in."

When I inquired of the agent where such things as mine should be exhibited, he said, "You see that building up on the hill with a big flag on it? That's the Fine Arts Hall, and it's just the place for your wonderful invention."

So I went up to the Fine Arts Hall and looked in, wondering if they would allow wooden things in so fine a place.

I was met at the door by a dignified gentleman, who greeted me kindly and said, "Young man, what have we got here?"

"Two clocks and a thermometer," I replied.

"Did you make these? They look wonderfully beautiful and novel and must, I think, prove the most interesting feature of the fair."

"Where shall I place them?" I inquired.

"Just look around, young man, and choose the place you like best, whether it is occupied or not. You can have your pick of all the building, and a carpenter to make the necessary shelving and assist you every way possible!"

So I quickly had a shelf made large enough for all of them, went out on the hill and picked up some glacial boulders of the right size for weights, and in fifteen or twenty minutes the clocks were running. They seemed to attract more attention than anything else in the Hall. I got lots of praise from the crowd and the newspaper reporters. The local press reports were copied into the eastern papers. It was considered wonderful that a boy on a farm had been able to invent and make such things, and almost every spectator foretold good fortune. But I had been so lectured by my father above all things to avoid praise that I was afraid to read those kind newspaper notices and never clipped out or preserved any of them, just glanced at them and turned away my eyes from beholding vanity. They gave me a prize of ten or fifteen dollars and a diploma for wonderful things not down in the list of exhibits.

Many years later, after I had written articles and books, I received a letter from the gentleman who had charge of the Fine Arts Hall. He proved to be the professor of English literature in the University of Wisconsin at this fair time, and long afterward he sent me clippings of reports of his lectures. He had a lecture on me, discussing style, etcetera, and telling how well he remembered my arrival at the Hall in my shirtsleeves with those mechanical wonders on my shoulder, and so forth, and so forth. These inventions, though of little importance, opened all doors for me and made marks that have lasted many years, simply, I suppose, because they were original and promising.

I was looking around in the mean time to find out where I should go to seek my fortune. An inventor at the fair, by the name of Wiard, was exhibiting an iceboat he had invented to run on the upper Mississippi from Prairie du Chien to St. Paul during the winter months, explaining how useful it would be thus to make a highway of the river while it was closed to ordinary navigation by ice. After he saw my inventions, he offered me a place in his foundry and machine shop in Prairie du Chien and promised to assist me all he could. So I made up my mind to accept his offer and rode with him to Prairie du Chien in his iceboat, which was mounted on a flat car. I soon found, however, that he was seldom at home and that I was not likely to learn much at his small shop. I found a place where I could work for my board and devote my spare hours to mechanical drawing, geometry, and physics, making but little headway, however, although the Pelton family, for whom I worked, were very kind. I made up my mind after a few months' stay in Prairie du Chien to return to Madison, hoping that in some way I might be able to gain an education.

At Madison I raised a few dollars by making and selling a few of those bedsteads that set the sleepers on their feet in the morning—inserting in the footboard the works of an ordinary clock that could be bought for a dollar. I also made a few dollars addressing circulars in an insurance office, while at the same time I was paying my board by taking care of a pair of horses and going errands. This is of no great interest except that I was thus winning my bread while hoping that something would turn up that might enable me to make money enough to enter the State University. This was my ambition, and it never wavered no matter what I was doing. No university, it seemed to me, could be more admirably situated, and as I sauntered about it, charmed with its fine lawns and trees and beautiful lakes, and saw the students going and coming with their books, and occasionally practicing with a theodolite in measuring distances, I thought that if I could only join them it would be the greatest joy of life. I was desperately hungry and thirsty for knowledge and willing to endure anything to get it.

One day I chanced to meet a student who had noticed my inventions at the fair and now recognized me. And when I said, "You are fortunate fellows to be allowed to study in this beautiful place. I wish I could join you," he asked, "Well, why don't you?" "I haven't money enough," I said. "Oh, as to money," he reassuringly explained, "very little is required. I presume you're able to enter the Freshman class, and you can board yourself as quite a number of us do at a cost of about a dollar a week. The baker and milkman come every day. You can live on bread and milk." Well, I thought, maybe

I have money enough for at least one beginning term. Anyhow I couldn't help trying.

With fear and trembling, overladen with ignorance, I called on Professor Stirling, the Dean of the Faculty, who was then Acting President, presented my case, and told him how far I had got on with my studies at home, and that I hadn't been to school since leaving Scotland at the age of eleven years, excepting one short term of a couple of months at a district school, because I could not be spared from the farm work. After hearing my story, the kind professor welcomed me to the glorious University—next, it seemed to me, to the Kingdom of Heaven. After a few weeks in the preparatory department, I entered the Freshman class. In Latin, I found that one of the books in use I had already studied in Scotland. So, after an interruption of a dozen years, I began my Latin over again where I had left off; and strange to say, most of it came back to me, especially the grammar which I had committed to memory at the Dunbar Grammar School.

During the four years that I was in the University, I earned enough in the harvest fields during the long summer vacations to carry me through the balance of each year, working very hard, cutting with a cradle four acres of wheat a day, and helping to put it in the shock. But, having to buy books and paying, I think, thirty-two dollars a year for instruction, and occasionally buying acids and retorts, glass tubing, bell-glasses, flasks, etc., I had to cut down expenses for board now and then to half a dollar a week.

One winter I taught school ten miles north of Madison, earning much-needed money at the rate of twenty dollars a month, "boarding 'round," and keeping up my University work by studying at night. As I was not then well enough off to own a watch, I used one of my hickory clocks, not only for keeping time, but for starting the school fire in the cold mornings, and regulating class times. I carried it out on my shoulder to the old log schoolhouse, and set it to work on a little shelf nailed to one of the knotty, bulging logs. The winter was very cold, and I had to go to the schoolhouse and start the fire about eight o'clock to warm it before the arrival of the scholars. This was a rather trying job, and one that my clock might easily be made to do. Therefore, after supper one evening I told the head of the family with whom I was boarding that if he would give me a candle I would go back to the schoolhouse and make arrangements for lighting the fire at eight o'clock, without my having to be present until time to open the school at nine. He said, "Oh! Young man, you have some curious things in the school room, but I don't think you can do that." I said, "Oh, yes! It's easy," and in hardly more than an hour, the simple job was completed. I had only to place a teaspoonful of powdered chlorate of potash and sugar on the stove-hearth near a few shavings and kindling, and at the required time make the clock, through a simple arrangement, touch the inflammable mixture with a drop of sulphuric acid. Every evening after school was dismissed, I shoveled out what was left of the fire into the snow, put in a little kindling, filled up the big box stove with heavy oak wood, placed the lighting arrangement on the hearth, and set the clock to drop the acid at the hour of eight; all of this requiring only a few minutes.

The first morning after I had made this simple arrangement, I invited the doubting farmer to watch the old squat schoolhouse from a window that overlooked it, to see if a good smoke did not rise from the stovepipe. Sure enough, on the minute, he saw a tall column curling gracefully up through the frosty air, but instead of congratulating me on my success he solemnly shook his head and said in a hollow, lugubrious voice, "Young man, you will be setting fire to the schoolhouse." All winter long that faithful clock fire never failed, and by the time I got to the schoolhouse the stove was usually red-hot.

At the beginning of the long summer vacations I returned to the Hickory Hill farm to earn the means in the harvest-fields to continue my University course, walking all the way to save railroad fares. And although I cradled four acres of wheat a day, I made the long, hard, sweaty day's work still longer and harder by keeping up my study of plants. At the noon hour I collected a large handful, put them in water to keep them fresh, and after supper got to work on them and sat up till after midnight, analyzing and classifying, thus leaving only four hours for sleep; and by the end of the first year, after taking up botany, I knew the principal flowering plants of the region.

I received my first lesson in botany from a student by the name of Griswold, who is now County Judge of the County of Waukesha, Wisconsin. In the university, he was often laughed at on account of his anxiety to instruct others and his frequently saying with fine emphasis, "Imparting instruction is my greatest enjoyment." One memorable day in June, when I was standing on the stone steps of the north dormitory, Mr. Griswold joined me and at once began to teach. He reached up, plucked a flower from an overspreading branch of a locust tree and, handing it to me, said, "Muir, do you know what family this tree belongs to?"

"No," I said, "I don't know anything about botany."

"Well, no matter," said he, "what is it like?"

"It's like a pea flower," I replied.

"That's right. You're right," he said. "It belongs to the pea family."

"But how can that be," I objected, "when the pea is a weak, clinging, straggling herb, and the locust a big, thorny hardwood tree?"

"Yes, that is true," he replied, "as to the difference in size, but it is also true that in all their essential characters they are alike, and therefore they must belong to one and the same family. Just look at the peculiar form of the locust flower; you see that the upper petal, called the banner, is broad and erect, and so is the upper petal of the pea flower. The two lower petals, called the wings, are outspread and wing-shaped; so are those of the pea. And the two petals below the wings are united on their edges, curve upward, and form what is called the keel, and so you see are the corresponding petals of the pea flower. And now look at the stamens and pistils. You see that nine of the ten stamens have their filaments united into a sheath around the pistil, but the tenth stamen has its filament free. These are very marked characters, are they not? And, strange to say, you will find them the same in the tree and in the vine. Now look at the ovules or seeds of the locust, and you will see that they are arranged in a pod or legume like those of the pea. And look at the leaves. You see the leaf of the locust is made up of several leaflets, and so also is the leaf of the pea. Now taste the locust leaf."

I did so and found that it tasted like the leaf of the pea. Nature has used the same seasoning for both, though one is a straggling vine, the other a big tree.

"Now, surely you cannot imagine that all these similar characters are mere coincidences. Do they not rather go to show that the Creator in making the pea vine and locust tree had the same idea in mind, and that plants are not classified arbitrarily? Man has nothing to do with their classification. Nature has attended to all that, giving essential unity with boundless variety, so that the botanist has only to examine plants to learn the harmony of their relations."

This fine lesson charmed me and sent me flying to the woods and meadows in wild enthusiasm. Like everybody else I was always fond of flowers, attracted by their external beauty and purity. Now my eyes were opened to their inner beauty, all alike revealing glorious traces of the thoughts of God, and leading on and on into the infinite cosmos. I wandered away at every opportunity, making long excursions round the lakes, gathering specimens, and keeping them fresh in a bucket in my room to study at night after my regular class tasks were learned, for my eyes never closed on the plant glory I had seen.

Nevertheless, I still indulged my love of mechanical inventions. I invented a desk in which the books I had to study were arranged in order at the beginning of each term. I also made a bed that set me on my feet every morning at the hour determined on, and in dark winter mornings just as the bed set me on the floor it lighted a lamp. Then, after the minutes allowed for dressing had elapsed, a click was heard and the first book to be studied was pushed up from a rack below the top of the desk, thrown open, and allowed to remain there the number of minutes required. Then the machinery closed the book and allowed it to drop back into its stall, then moved the rack forward and threw up the next in order, and so on, all the day being divided according to the times of recitation, and time required and allotted to each study. Besides this, I thought it would be a fine thing in the summertime when the sun rose early, to dispense with the clock-controlled bed machinery and make use of sunbeams instead. This I did simply by taking a lens out of my small spyglass, fixing it on a frame on the sill of my bedroom window, and pointing it to the sunrise; the sunbeams focused on a thread burned it through, allowing the bed machinery to put me on my feet. When I wished to arise at any given time after sunrise, I had only to turn the pivoted frame that held the lens the requisite number of degrees or minutes. Thus I took Emerson's advice and hitched my dumping-wagon bed to a star.

I also invented a machine to make visible the growth of plants and the action of the sunlight, a very delicate contrivance, enclosed in glass. Besides this I invented a barometer and a lot of novel scientific apparatus. My room was regarded as a sort of show place by the professors, who oftentimes brought visitors to it on Saturdays and holidays. And when, some eighteen years after I had left the University, I was sauntering over the campus in time of vacation, and spoke to a man who seemed to be taking some charge of the grounds, he informed me that he was the janitor; and when I inquired what had become of Pat, the janitor in my time and a favorite with the students, he replied that Pat was still alive and well, but now too old to do much work. And when I pointed to the dormitory room that I long ago occupied, he said: "Oh! Then I know who you are," and mentioned my name. "How comes it that you know my name?" I inquired. He explained that "Pat always pointed out that room to newcomers and told long stories about the wonders that used to be in it." So long had the memory of my little inventions survived.

Although I was four years at the University, I did not take the regular course of studies, but instead picked out what I thought would be most useful to me, particularly chemistry, which opened a new world, and mathematics and physics, a little Greek and Latin, botany and geology. I was far from satisfied with what I had learned, and should have stayed longer. Anyhow I wandered away on a glorious botanical and geological excursion, which has lasted nearly fifty years and is not yet completed, always happy and free, poor and rich, without thought of a diploma or of making a name, urged on and on through endless, inspiring, Godful beauty.

From the top of a hill on the north side of Lake Mendota I gained a last wistful, lingering view of the beautiful university grounds and buildings where I had spent so many hungry and happy and hopeful days. There with streaming eyes I bade my blessed alma mater farewell. But I was only leaving one university for another, the Wisconsin University for the University of the Wilderness.

PART TWO:

The Wandering Minstrel

Through the Cumberland Mountains, the River Country of Georgia, and across Florida to Cedar Keys

SEPTEMBER 12.

Awoke drenched with mountain mist, which made a grand show, as it moved away before the hot sun. Passed Montgomery, a shabby village at the head of the east slope of the Cumberland Mountains. Obtained breakfast in a clean house and began the descent of the mountains. Obtained fine views of a wide, open country, and distant flanking ridges and spurs. Crossed a wide cool stream [Emory River], a branch of the Clinch River. There is nothing more eloquent in nature than a mountain stream, and this is the first I ever saw. Its banks are luxuriantly peopled with rare and lovely flowers and overarching trees, making one of Nature's coolest and most hospitable places. Every tree, every flower, every ripple and eddy of this lovely stream seemed solemnly to feel the presence of the great Creator. Lingered in this sanctuary a long time, thanking the Lord with all my heart for his goodness in allowing me to enter and enjoy it.

Discovered two ferns, *Dicksonia* and a small matted polypod on trees, common farther south. Also a species of magnolia with very large leaves and scarlet conical fruit. Near this stream I spent some joyous time in a grand rock dwelling full of mosses, birds, and flowers. Most heavenly place I ever entered. The long, narrow valleys of the mountainside, all well watered and nobly adorned with oaks, magnolias, laurels, azaleas, asters, ferns, *Hypnum* mosses, *Madotheca* [scale mosses], etc. Also towering clumps of beautiful hemlocks. The hemlock, judging from the common species of Canada, I regarded as the least noble of the conifers. But those of the eastern valleys of the Cumberland Mountains are as perfect in form and regal in port as the pines themselves. The latter abundant. Obtained fine glimpses from open places as I descended to the great valley between these mountains and the Unaka Mountains on the state line. Forded the Clinch, a, beautiful clear stream that knows many of the dearest mountain retreats that ever heard the music of running water. Reached Kingston before dark. Sent back my plant collections by express to my brother in Wisconsin.

SEPTEMBER 13.

Walked all day across small parallel valleys that flute the surface of the one wide valley. These flutings appear to have been formed by lateral pressure, are fertile, and contain some fine forms, though the seal of war is on all things. The roads never seem to proceed with any fixed purpose, but wander as if lost. In seeking the way to Philadelphia [in Loudon County, Tennessee], I was told by a buxom Tennessee "gal" that over the hills was much the nearer way, that she always went that way, and that surely I could travel it.

I started over the flint ridges, but soon reached a set of enchanted little valleys among which, no matter how or in what direction I traveled, I could not get a foot nearer to Philadelphia. At last, consulting my map and compass, I neglected all directions and finally reached the house of a Negro driver, with whom I put up for the night. Received a good deal of knowledge which may be of use should I ever be a Negro teamster.

SEPTEMBER 14.

Philadelphia is a very filthy village in a beautiful situation. More or less of pine. Black oak most abundant. *Polypodium hexagonopterum* and *Aspidium acrostichoides* [Christmas fern] most abundant of ferns and most generally distributed. *Osmunda claytoniana* rare, not in fruit, small. *Dicksonia* abundant after leaving the Cumberland Mountains. *Asplenium ebeneum* [ebony spleenwort] quite common in Tennessee and many parts of Kentucky. *Cystopteris* [bladder fern], and *Aspleniumfilix foemina* not common through the same range. *Pteris aquilina* [common brake] abundant, but small.

Walked through many a leafy valley, shady grove, and cool brooklet. Reached Madisonville, a brisk village. Came in full view of the Unaka Mountains, a magnificent sight. Stayed overnight with a pleasant young farmer.

The River Country of Georgia

OCTOBER 3.

In "pine barrens" most of the day. Low, level, sandy tracts; the pines wide apart; the sunny spaces between full of beautiful abounding grasses, *Liatris*, long, wandlike *Solidago*, saw palmettos, etc., covering the ground in garden style. Here I sauntered in delightful freedom, meeting none of the cat-clawed vines, or shrubs, of the alluvial bottoms. Dwarf live oaks common.

Toward evening I arrived at the home of Mr. Cameron, a wealthy planter, who had large bands of slaves at work in his cotton fields. They still call him "Massa." He tells me that labor costs him less now than it did before the emancipation of the Negroes. When I arrived I found him busily engaged in scouring the rust off some cotton-gin saws which had been lying for months at the bottom of his millpond to prevent Sherman's "bummers" from destroying them. The most valuable parts of the gristmill and cotton press were hidden in the same way. "If Bill Sherman," he said, "should come down now without his army, he would never go back."

When I asked him if he could give me food and lodging for the night he said, "No, no, we have no accommodations for travelers." I said, "But I am traveling as a botanist and either have to find lodgings when night overtakes me or lie outdoors, which I often have had to do in my long walk from Indiana. But you see that the country here is very swampy. If you will at least sell me a piece of bread and give me a drink at your well, I shall have to look around for a dry spot to lie down on."

Then, asking me a few questions, and narrowly examining me, he said, "Well, it is barely possible that we may find a place for you, and if you will come to the house I will ask my wife." Evidently he was cautious to get his wife's opinion of the kind of creature I was before committing himself to hospitality. He halted me at the door and called out his wife, a fine-looking woman, who also questioned me narrowly as to my object in coming so far down through the South, so soon after the war. She said to her husband that she thought they could, perhaps, give me a place to sleep.

After supper, as we sat by the fire talking on my favorite subject of botany, I described the country I had passed through, its botanical character, etc. Then, evidently, all doubt as to my being a decent man vanished, and they both said that they wouldn't for anything have turned me away; but I must excuse their caution, for perhaps fewer than one in a hundred, who passed through this unfrequented part of the country were to be relied upon. "Only a short time ago we entertained a man who was well spoken and well dressed, and he vanished some time during the night with some valuable silverware."

Mr. Cameron told me that when I arrived he tried me for a Mason, and finding that I was not a Mason he wondered still more that I would venture into the country without being able to gain the assistance of brother Masons in these troublous times.

"Young man," he said, after hearing my talks on botany, "I see that your hobby is botany. My hobby is e-lec-tricity. I believe that the time is coming, though we may not live to see it, when that mysterious power or force, used now only for telegraphy, will eventually supply the power for running railroad trains and steamships, for lighting and, in a word, electricity will do all the work of the world."

Many times since then I have thought of the wonderfully correct vision of this Georgia planter, so far in advance of almost everybody else in the world. Already nearly all that he foresaw has been accomplished, and the use of electricity is being extended more and more every year.

OCTOBER 4.
New plants constantly appearing. All day in dense, wet, dark, mysterious forest of flat-topped *Taxodiums.*

Cedar Keys

OCTOBER 23.

Today I reached the sea. While I was yet many miles back in the palmy woods, I caught the scent of the salt sea breeze which, although I had so many years lived far from sea breezes, suddenly conjured up Dunbar, its rocky coast, winds and waves; and my whole childhood, which seemed to have utterly vanished in the New World, was now restored amid the Florida woods by that one breath from the sea. Forgotten were the palms and magnolias and the thousand flowers that enclosed me. I could see only dulse and tangle, long-winged gulls, the Bass Rock in the Firth of Forth, and the old castle, schools, churches, and long country rambles in search of birds' nests. I do not wonder that the weary camels coming from the scorching African deserts should be able to scent the Nile.

How imperishable are all the impressions that ever vibrate one's life! We cannot forget anything. Memories may escape the action of will, may sleep a long time, but when stirred by the right influence, though that influence be light as a shadow, they flash into full stature and life with everything in place. For nineteen years my vision was bounded by forests, but today, emerging from a multitude of tropical plants, I beheld the Gulf of Mexico stretching away unbounded, except by the sky. What dreams and speculative matter for thought arose as I stood on the strand, gazing out on the burnished, treeless plain!

But now at the seaside I was in difficulty. I had reached a point that I could not ford, and Cedar Keys had an empty harbor. Would I proceed down the peninsula to Tampa and Key West, where I would be sure to find a vessel for Cuba, or would I wait here, like Crusoe, and pray for a ship. Full of these thoughts, I stepped into a little store which had a considerable trade in quinine and alligator and rattlesnake skins, and inquired about shipping, means of travel, etc.

The proprietor informed me that one of several sawmills near the village was running, and that a schooner chartered to carry a load of lumber to Galveston, Texas, was expected at the mills for a load. This mill was situated on a tongue of land a few miles along the coast from Cedar Keys, and I determined to see Mr. Hodgson, the owner, to find out particulars about the expected schooner, the time she would take to load, whether I would be likely to obtain passage on her, etc.

Found Mr. Hodgson at his mill. Stated my case, and was kindly furnished the desired information. I determined to wait the two weeks likely to elapse before she sailed, and go on her to the flowery plains of Texas, from any of whose ports, I fancied, I could easily find passage to the West Indies. I agreed to work for Mr. Hodgson in the mill until I sailed, as I had but little money. He invited me to his spacious house, which occupied a shell hillock and commanded a fine view of the Gulf and many gems of palmy islets, called "keys," that fringe the shore like huge bouquets—not too big, however, for the spacious waters. Mr. Hodgson's family welcomed me with that open, unconstrained cordiality which is characteristic of the better class of Southern people.

At the sawmill a new cover had been put on the main driving pulley, which, made of rough plank, had to be turned off and smoothed. He asked me if I was able to do this job, and I told him that I could. Fixing a rest and making a tool out of an old file, I directed the engineer to start the engine and run slow. After turning down the pulley and getting it true, I put a keen edge on a common carpenter's plane, quickly finished the job, and was assigned a bunk in one of the employees' lodging houses.

The next day I felt a strange dullness and headache while I was botanizing along the coast. Thinking that a bath in the salt water might refresh me, I plunged in and swam a little distance, but this seemed only to make me feel worse. I felt anxious for something sour, and walked back to the village to buy lemons.

Thus and here my long walk was interrupted. I thought that a few days' sail would land me among the famous flower beds of Texas. But the expected ship came and went while I was helpless with fever. The very day after reaching the sea I began to be weighed down by inexorable leaden numbness, which I resisted and tried to shake off for three days, by bathing in the Gulf, by dragging myself about among the palms, plants, and strange shells of the shore, and by doing a little mill work. I did not fear any serious illness, for I never was sick before and was unwilling to pay attention to my feelings.

But yet heavier and more remorselessly pressed the growing fever, rapidly gaining on my strength. On the third day after my arrival I could not take any nourishment, but craved acid. Cedar Keys was only a mile or two distant, and I managed to walk there to buy lemons. On returning, about the middle of the afternoon, the fever broke on me like a storm, and before I had staggered halfway to the mill I fell down unconscious on the narrow trail among dwarf palmettos.

When I awoke from the hot fever sleep, the stars were shining and I was at a loss to know which end of the trail to take, but fortunately, as it afterwards proved, I guessed right. Subsequently, as I fell again and again after walking only a hundred yards or so, I was careful to lie with my head in the direction in which I thought the mill was. I rose, staggered, and fell, I know not how many times, in delirious bewilderment, gasping and throbbing with only moments of consciousness. Thus passed the hours till after midnight, when I reached the mill lodging house.

The watchman on his rounds found me lying on a heap of sawdust at the foot of the stairs. I asked him to assist me up the steps to bed, but he thought my difficulty was only intoxication and refused to help me. The mill hands, especially on Saturday nights, often returned from the village drunk. This was the cause of the watchman's refusal. Feeling that I must get to bed, I made out to reach it on hands and knees, tumbled in after a desperate struggle, and immediately became oblivious to everything.

I awoke at a strange hour on a strange day to hear Mr. Hodgson ask a watcher beside me whether I had yet spoken, and when he replied that I had not, he said: "Well, you must keep on pouring in quinine. That's all we can do." How long I lay unconscious I never found out, but it must have been many days. Some time or other I was moved on a horse from the mill quarters to Mr. Hodgson's house, where I was nursed about three months with unfailing kindness, and to the skill and care of Mr. and Mrs. Hodgson I doubtless owe my life. Through quinine and calomel—in sorry abundance—with other milder medicines, my malarial fever became typhoid. I had night sweats, and my legs became like posts of the temper and consistency of clay on account of dropsy. So on until January, a weary time.

As soon as I was able to get out of bed, I crept away to the edge
of the wood and sat, day after day, beneath a moss-draped live oak,
watching birds feeding on the shore when the tide was out. Later,
as I gathered some strength, I sailed in a little skiff from one key
to another. Nearly all the shrubs and trees here are evergreen, and
a few of the smaller plants are in flower all winter. The principal
trees on this Cedar Key are the juniper, long-leafed pine, and live
oak. All of the latter, living and dead, are heavily draped with
Tillandsia, like those of Bonaventure. The leaf is oval, about two
inches long, three-fourths of an inch wide, glossy and dark green
above, pale beneath. The trunk is usually much-divided, and is
extremely unwedgeable. The specimen on the opposite page [of
the original journal] is growing in the dooryard of Mr. Hodgson's
house. It is a grand old king, whose crown gleamed in the bright
sky long ere the Spanish shipbuilders felled a single tree of this
noble species.

The live oaks of these keys divide empire with the long-leafed
pine and palmetto, but in many places on the mainland there are
large tracts exclusively occupied by them. Like the Bonaventure
oaks, they have the upper side of their main spreading branches
thickly planted with ferns, grasses, small saw palmettos, etc. There
is also a dwarf oak here, which forms dense thickets. The oaks of
this key are not, like those of the Wisconsin openings, growing on
grassy slopes, but stand, sunk to the shoulders, in flowering magnolias, heathworts, etc.

During my long sojourn here as a convalescent I used to lie on
my back for whole days beneath the ample arms of these great
trees, listening to the winds and the birds. There is an extensive
shallow on the coast, close by, which the receding tide exposes
daily. This is the feeding-ground of thousands of waders of all
sizes, plumage, and language, and they make a lively picture and
noise when they gather at the great family board to eat their daily
bread, so bountifully provided for them.

Their leisure in time of high tide they spend in various ways and
places. Some go in large flocks to reedy margins about the islands
and wade and stand about quarreling or making sport, occasionally
finding a stray mouthful to eat. Some stand on the mangroves of the
solitary shore, now and then plunging into the water after a fish.

Some go long journeys inland, up creeks and inlets. A few lonely old herons of solemn look and wing retire to favorite oaks. It was my delight to watch those old white sages of immaculate feather as they stood erect drowsing away the dull hours between tides, curtained by long skeins of *Tillandsia*. White-bearded hermits gazing dreamily from dark caves could not appear more solemn or more becomingly shrouded from the rest of their fellow beings.

One of the characteristic plants of these keys is the Spanish bayonet, a species of *Yucca*, about eight or ten feet in height, and with a trunk three or four inches in diameter when full-grown. It belongs to the lily family and develops palm-like from terminal buds. The stout leaves are very rigid, sharp-pointed, and bayonet-like. By one of these leaves a man might be as seriously stabbed as by an army bayonet, and woe to the luckless wanderer who dares to urge his way through these armed gardens after dark. Vegetable cats of many species will rob him of his clothes and claw his flesh, while dwarf palmettos will saw his bones, and the bayonets will glide to his joints and marrow without the smallest consideration for Lord Man.

The climate of these precious islets is simply warm summer and warmer summer, corresponding in time with winter and summer in the North. The weather goes smoothly over the points of union betwixt the twin summers. Few of the storms are very loud or variable. The average temperature during the day, in December, was about sixty-five degrees in the shade, but on one day a little damp snow fell.

Cedar Key is two-and-one-half or three miles in diameter, and its highest point is forty-four feet above mean tidewater. It is surrounded by scores of other keys, many of them looking like a clump of palms, arranged like a tasteful bouquet, and placed in the sea to be kept fresh. Others have quite a sprinkling of oaks and junipers, beautifully united with vines. Still others consist of shells, with a few grasses and mangroves, circled with a rim of rushes. Those which have sedgy margins furnish a favorite retreat for countless waders and divers, especially for the pelicans that frequently whiten the shore like a ring of foam.

It is delightful to observe the assembling of these feathered people from the woods and reedy isles; herons white as wave-tops, or blue as the sky, winnowing the warm air on wide, quiet wing; pelicans coming with baskets to fill, and the multitude of smaller sailors of the air, swift as swallows, gracefully taking their places at Nature's family table for their daily bread. Happy birds!

PART THREE:

The Nature Scribe and Rhapsode

A Near View of the High Sierra

Early one bright morning in the middle of Indian summer, while the glacier meadows were still crisp with frost crystals, I set out from the foot of Mount Lyell on my way down to Yosemite Valley, to replenish my exhausted store of bread and tea. I had spent the past summer, as many preceding ones, exploring the glaciers that lie on the head waters of the San Joaquin, Tuolumne, Merced, and Owen's rivers; measuring and studying their movements, trends, crevasses, moraines, etc., and the part they had played during the period of their greater extension in the creation and development of the landscapes of this alpine wonderland. The time for this kind of work was nearly over for the year, and I began to look forward with delight to the approaching winter with its wondrous storms, when I would be warmly snowbound in my Yosemite cabin with plenty of bread and books; but a tinge of regret came on when I considered that possibly I might not see this favorite region again until the next summer, excepting distant views from the heights about the Yosemite walls.

To artists, few portions of the High Sierra are, strictly speaking, picturesque. The whole massive uplift of the range is one great picture, not clearly divisible into smaller ones; differing much in this respect from the older, and what may be called, riper mountains of the Coast Range. All the landscapes of the Sierra, as we have seen, were born again, remodeled from base to summit by the developing ice floods of the last glacial winter. But all these new landscapes were not brought forth simultaneously; some of the highest, where the ice lingered longest, are tens of centuries younger than those of the warmer regions below them. In general, the younger the mountain landscapes—younger, I mean, with reference to the time of their emergence from the ice of the glacial period—the less separable are they into artistic bits capable of being made into warm, sympathetic, lovable pictures with appreciable humanity in them.

Here, however, on the head waters of the Tuolumne, is a group of wild peaks on which the geologist may say that the sun has but just begun to shine, which is yet in a high degree picturesque, and in its main features so regular and evenly balanced as almost to appear conventional—one somber cluster of snow-laden peaks with gray pine-fringed granite bosses braided around its base, the whole surging free into the sky from the head of a magnificent valley, whose lofty walls are beveled away on both sides so as to embrace it all without admitting anything not strictly belonging to it. The foreground was now aflame with autumn colors, brown and purple and gold, ripe in the mellow sunshine; contrasting brightly with the deep, cobalt blue of the sky, and the black and gray, and pure, spiritual white of the rocks and glaciers. Down through the midst, the young Tuolumne was seen pouring from its crystal fountains, now resting in glassy pools as if changing back again into ice, now leaping in white cascades as if turning to snow; gliding right and left between granite bosses, then sweeping on through the smooth, meadowy levels of the valley, swaying pensively from side to side with calm, stately gestures past dipping willows and sedges, and around groves of arrowy pine; and throughout its whole eventful course, whether flowing fast or slow, singing loud or low, ever filling the landscape with spiritual animation, and manifesting the grandeur of its sources in every movement and tone.

Pursuing my lonely way down the valley, I turned again and again to gaze on the glorious picture, throwing up my arms to enclose it as in a frame. After long ages of growth in the darkness beneath the glaciers, through sunshine and storms, it seemed now to be ready and waiting for the elected artist, like yellow wheat for the reaper; and I could not help wishing that I might carry colors and brushes with me on my travels, and learn to paint. In the mean time I had to be content with photographs on my mind and sketches in my notebooks. At length, after I had rounded a precipitous headland that puts out from the west wall of the valley, every peak vanished from sight, and I pushed rapidly along the frozen meadows, over the divide between the waters of the Merced and

Tuolumne, and down through the forests that clothe the slopes of Cloud's Rest, arriving in Yosemite in due time—which, with me, is any time. And, strange to say, among the first people I met here were two artists who, with letters of introduction, were awaiting my return. They inquired whether in the course of my explorations in the adjacent mountains I had ever come upon a landscape suitable for a large painting; whereupon I began a description of the one that had so lately excited my admiration. Then, as I went on further and further into details, their faces began to glow, and I offered to guide them to it, while they declared that they would gladly follow, far or near, whithersoever I could spare the time to lead them.

Since storms might come breaking down through the fine weather at any time, burying the colors in snow and cutting off the artists' retreat, I advised getting ready at once. I led them out of the valley by the Vernal and Nevada Falls, thence over the main dividing ridge to the Big Tuolumne Meadows, by the old Mono trail, and thence along the upper Tuolumne River to its head. This was my companions' first excursion into the High Sierra, and as I was almost always alone in my mountaineering, the way that the fresh beauty was reflected in their faces made for me a novel and interesting study. They naturally were affected most of all by the colors: the intense azure of the sky, the purplish grays of the granite, the red and browns of dry meadows, and the translucent purple and crimson of huckleberry bogs; the flaming yellow of aspen groves, the silvery flashing of the streams, and the bright green and blue of the glacier lakes. But the general expression of the scenery—rocky and savage—seemed sadly disappointing; and as they threaded the forest from ridge to ridge, eagerly scanning the landscapes as they were unfolded, they said: "All this is huge and sublime, but we see nothing as yet at all available for effective pictures. Art is long, and art is limited, you know; and here are foregrounds, middle-grounds, backgrounds, all alike; bare rock-waves, woods, groves, diminutive flecks of meadow, and strips of glittering water." "Never mind," I replied, "only bide a wee, and I will show you something you will like."

At length, toward the end of the second day, the Sierra Crown began to come into view, and when we had fairly rounded the projecting headland before mentioned, the whole picture stood revealed in the flush of the alpenglow. Their enthusiasm was excited beyond bounds, and the more impulsive of the two, a young Scotchman, dashed ahead, shouting and gesticulating and tossing his arms in the air like a madman. Here, at last, was a typical alpine landscape.

After feasting awhile on the view, I proceeded to make camp in a sheltered grove a little way back from the meadow, where pine boughs could be obtained for beds, and where there was plenty of dry wood for fires, while the artists ran here and there, along the river bends and up the sides of the canyon, choosing foregrounds for sketches. After dark, when our tea was made and a rousing fire had been built, we began to make our plans. They decided to remain several days, at the least, while I concluded to make an excursion in the mean time to the untouched summit of Ritter.

It was now about the middle of October, the springtime of snow flowers. The first winter clouds had already bloomed, and the peaks were strewn with fresh crystals, without, however, affecting the climbing to any dangerous extent. And as the weather was still profoundly calm, and the distance to the foot of the mountain only a little more than a day, I felt that I was running no great risk of being storm-bound.

Mount Ritter is king of the mountains of the middle portion of the High Sierra, as Shasta of the north and Whitney of the south sections. Moreover, as far as I know, it had never been climbed. I had explored the adjacent wilderness summer after summer, but my studies thus far had never drawn me to the top of it. Its height above sea level is about 13,300 feet, and it is fenced 'round by steeply inclined glaciers, and canyons of tremendous depth and ruggedness, which render it almost inaccessible. But difficulties of this kind only exhilarate the mountaineer.

Next morning, the artists went heartily to their work and I to mine. Former experiences had given good reason to know that passionate storms, invisible as yet, might be brooding in the calm sun-gold; therefore, before bidding farewell, I warned the artists not to be alarmed should I fail to appear before a week or ten days, and advised them, in case a snowstorm should set in, to keep up big fires

and shelter themselves as best they could, and on no account to
become frightened and attempt to seek their way back to Yosemite
alone through the drifts.

My general plan was simply this: to scale the canyon wall, cross
over to the eastern flank of the range, and then make my way
southward to the northern spurs of Mount Ritter in compliance
with the intervening topography; for to push on directly southward from camp through the innumerable peaks and pinnacles
that adorn this portion of the axis of the range, however interesting, would take too much time, besides being extremely difficult
and dangerous at this time of year.

All my first day was pure pleasure; simply mountaineering
indulgence, crossing the dry pathways of the ancient glaciers,
tracing happy streams, and learning the habits of the birds and
marmots in the groves and rocks. Before I had gone a mile from
camp, I came to the foot of a white cascade that beats its way down
a rugged gorge in the canyon wall, from a height of about nine
hundred feet, and pours its throbbing waters into the Tuolumne.
I was acquainted with its fountains, which, fortunately, lay in my
course. What a fine traveling companion it proved to be, what
songs it sang, and how passionately it told the mountain's own joy!
Gladly I climbed along its dashing border, absorbing its divine
music, and bathing from time to time in waftings of irised spray.
Climbing higher, higher, new beauty came streaming on the sight:
painted meadows, late-blooming gardens, peaks of rare architecture, lakes here and there, shining like silver, and glimpses of the
forested middle region and the yellow lowlands far in the west.
Beyond the range I saw the so-called Mono Desert, lying dreamily
silent in thick purple light—a desert of heavy sun-glare beheld
from a desert of ice-burnished granite. Here the waters divide,
shouting in glorious enthusiasm, and falling eastward to vanish in
the volcanic sands and dry sky of the Great Basin, or westward to
the Great Valley of California, and thence through the Bay of San
Francisco and the Golden Gate to the sea.

Passing a little way down over the summit until I had reached an
elevation of about ten thousand feet, I pushed on southward toward
a group of savage peaks that stand guard about Ritter on the north

and west, groping my way, and dealing instinctively with every obstacle as it presented itself. Here a huge gorge would be found cutting across my path, along the dizzy edge of which I scrambled until some less precipitous point was discovered where I might safely venture to the bottom and then, selecting some feasible portion of the opposite wall, reascend with the same slow caution. Massive, flat-topped spurs alternate with the gorges, plunging abruptly from the shoulders of the snowy peaks, and planting their feet in the warm desert. These were everywhere marked and adorned with characteristic sculptures of the ancient glaciers that swept over this entire region like one vast ice-wind, and the polished surfaces produced by the ponderous flood are still so perfectly preserved that in many places the sunlight reflected from them is about as trying to the eyes as sheets of snow.

God's glacial-mills grind slowly, but they have been kept in motion long enough in California to grind sufficient soil for a glorious abundance of life, though most of the grist has been carried to the lowlands, leaving these high regions comparatively lean and bare; while the postglacial agents of erosion have not yet furnished sufficient available food over the general surface for more than a few tufts of the hardiest plants, chiefly carices and eriogonae. And it is interesting to learn in this connection that the sparseness and repressed character of the vegetation at this height is caused more by want of soil than by harshness of climate; for here and there, in sheltered hollows (countersunk beneath the general surface) into which a few rods of well ground moraine chips have been dumped, we find groves of spruce and pine thirty to forty feet high, trimmed around the edges with willow and huckleberry bushes, and oftentimes still farther by an outer ring of tall grasses, bright with lupines, larkspurs, and showy columbines, suggesting a climate by no means repressingly severe. All the streams, too, and the pools at this elevation are furnished with little gardens wherever soil can be made to lie, which, though making scarce any show at a distance, constitute charming surprises to the appreciative observer. In these bits of leafiness a few birds find grateful homes. Having no acquaintance with man, they fear no ill, and flock curiously about the stranger, almost allowing themselves to be taken in the hand.

In so wild and so beautiful a region was spent my first day, every sight and sound inspiring, leading one far out of himself, yet feeding and building up his individuality.

Now came the solemn, silent evening. Long, blue, spiky shadows crept out across the snowfields, while a rosy glow, at first scarce discernible, gradually deepened and suffused every mountaintop, flushing the glaciers and the harsh crags above them. This was the alpenglow, to me one of the most impressive of all the terrestrial manifestations of God. At the touch of this divine light, the mountains seemed to kindle to a rapt, religious consciousness, and stood hushed and waiting like devout worshipers. Just before the alpenglow began to fade, two crimson clouds came streaming across the summit like wings of flame, rendering the sublime scene yet more impressive; then came darkness and the stars.

Icy Ritter was still miles away, but I could proceed no farther that night. I found a good campground on the rim of a glacier basin about eleven thousand feet above the sea. A small lake nestles in the bottom of it, from which I got water for my tea, and a storm-beaten thicket nearby furnished abundance of resiny firewood. Somber peaks, hacked and shattered, circled halfway around the horizon, wearing a savage aspect in the gloaming, and a waterfall chanted solemnly across the lake on its way down from the foot of a glacier. The fall and the lake and the glacier were almost equally bare; while the scraggy pines anchored in the rock fissures were so dwarfed and shorn by storm winds that you might walk over their tops. In tone and aspect the scene was one of the most desolate I ever beheld. But the darkest scriptures of the mountains are illumined with bright passages of love that never fail to make themselves felt when one is alone.

I made my bed in a nook of the pine-thicket, where the branches were pressed and crinkled overhead like a roof, and bent down around the sides. These are the best bedchambers the high mountains afford—snug as squirrel nests, well ventilated, full of spicy odors, and with plenty of wind-played needles to sing one asleep. I little expected company, but, creeping in through a low side door, I found five or six birds nestling among the tassels. The night wind began to blow soon after dark; at first only a gentle breathing, but increasing toward midnight to a rough gale that fell upon my leafy roof in ragged surges like a cascade, bearing wild sounds from the crags overhead. The waterfall sang in chorus, filling the old ice fountain with its solemn roar, and seeming to increase in power as the night advanced—fit voice for such a landscape. I had to creep out many times to the fire during the night, for it was biting cold and I had no blankets. Gladly I welcomed the morning star.

The dawn in the dry, wavering air of the desert was glorious. Everything encouraged my undertaking and betokened success. There was no cloud in the sky, no storm tone in the wind. Breakfast of bread and tea was soon made. I fastened a hard, durable crust to my belt by way of provision, in case I should be compelled to pass a night on the mountaintop; then, securing the remainder of my little stock against wolves and wood rats, I set forth free and hopeful.

How glorious a greeting the sun gives the mountains! To behold this alone is worth the pains of any excursion a thousand times over. The highest peaks burned like islands in a sea of liquid shade. Then the lower peaks and spires caught the glow, and long lances of light, streaming through many a notch and pass, fell thick on the frozen meadows. The majestic form of Ritter was full in sight, and I pushed rapidly on over rounded rock bosses and pavements, my iron-shod shoes making a clanking sound, suddenly hushed now and then in rugs of *Bryanthus*, and sedgy lake margins soft as moss. Here, too, in this so-called "land of desolation," I met *Cassiope*, growing in fringes among the battered rocks. Her blossoms had faded long ago, but they were still clinging with happy memories to the evergreen sprays, and still so beautiful as to thrill every fiber of one's being. Winter and summer, you may hear her voice, the low, sweet melody of her purple bells. No evangel among all the mountain plants speaks Nature's love more plainly than *Cassiope*. Where she dwells, the redemption of the coldest solitude is complete. The very rocks and glaciers seem to feel her presence, and become imbued with her own fountain sweetness. All things were warming and awakening. Frozen rills began to flow, the marmots came out of their nests in boulder piles and climbed sunny rocks to bask, and the dun-headed sparrows were flitting about seeking their breakfasts. The lakes seen from every ridgetop were brilliantly rippled and spangled, shimmering like the thickets of the low dwarf pines. The rocks, too, seemed responsive to the vital heat—rock crystals and snow crystals thrilling alike. I strode on exhilarated, as if never more to feel fatigue, limbs moving of themselves, every sense unfolding like the thawing flowers, to take part in the new day harmony.

All along my course thus far, excepting when down in the canyons, the landscapes were mostly open to me, and expansive, at least on one side. On the left were the purple plains of Mono, reposing dreamily and warm; on the right, the near peaks springing keenly into the thin sky with more and more impressive sublimity. But these larger views were at length lost. Rugged spurs, and moraines, and huge, projecting buttresses began to shut me in. Every feature became more rigidly alpine, without, however, producing any chilling effect; for going to the mountains is like going home. We always find that the strangest objects in these fountain wilds are in some degree familiar, and we look upon them with a vague sense of having seen them before.

On the southern shore of a frozen lake, I encountered an extensive field of hard, granular snow, up which I scampered in fine tone, intending to follow it to its head, and cross the rocky spur against which it leans, hoping thus to come direct upon the base of the main Ritter peak. The surface was pitted with oval hollows, made by stones and drifted pine needles that had melted themselves into the mass by the radiation of absorbed sun heat. These afforded good footholds, but the surface curved more and more steeply at the head, and the pits became shallower and less abundant, until I found myself in danger of being shed off like avalanching snow. I persisted, however, creeping on all fours, and shuffling up the smoothest places on my back, as I had often done on burnished granite, until, after slipping several times, I was compelled to retrace my course to the bottom, and make my way around the west end of the lake, and thence up to the summit of the divide between the head waters of Rush Creek and the northernmost tributaries of the San Joaquin.

Arriving on the summit of this dividing crest, one of the most exciting pieces of pure wilderness was disclosed that I ever discovered in all my mountaineering. There, immediately in front, loomed the majestic mass of Mount Ritter, with a glacier swooping down its face nearly to my feet, then curving westward and pouring its frozen flood into a dark blue lake, whose shores were bound with precipices of crystalline snow; while a deep chasm drawn between the divide and the glacier separated the massive picture from everything else. I could see only the one sublime mountain, the one glacier, the one lake; the whole veiled with one blue shadow-rock, ice, and water close together without a single leaf or sign of life. After gazing spellbound, I began instinctively to scrutinize every notch and gorge and weathered buttress of the mountain, with reference to making the ascent. The entire front above the glacier appeared as one tremendous precipice, slightly receding at the top, and bristling with spires and pinnacles set above one another in formidable array. Massive lichen-stained battlements stood forward here and there, hacked at the top with angular notches, and separated by frosty gullies and recesses that have been veiled in shadow ever since their creation; while to right and left, as far as I could see, were huge, crumbling buttresses, offering no hope to the climber. The head of the glacier sends up a few finger-like branches through narrow couloir, but these seemed too steep and short to be available, especially as I had no ax with which to cut steps, and the numerous narrow-throated gullies down which stones and snow are avalanched seemed hopelessly steep, besides being interrupted by vertical cliffs; while the whole front was rendered still more terribly forbidding by the chill shadow and the gloomy blackness of the rocks.

Descending the divide in a hesitating mood, I picked my way across the yawning chasm at the foot and climbed out upon the glacier. There were no meadows now to cheer with their brave colors, nor could I hear the dun-headed sparrows, whose cheery notes so often relieve the silence of our highest mountains. The only sounds were the gurgling of small rills down in the veins and crevasses of the glacier, and now and then the rattling report of falling stones, with the echoes they shot out into the crisp air.

I could not distinctly hope to reach the summit from this side, yet I moved on across the glacier as if driven by fate. Contending with myself, the season is too far spent, I said, and even should I be successful, I might be stormbound on the mountain; and in the cloud darkness, with the cliffs and crevasses covered with snow, how could I escape? No; I must wait till next summer. I would only approach the mountain now, and inspect it, creep about its flanks, learn what I could of its history, holding myself ready to flee on the approach of the first storm cloud. But we little know until tried how much of the uncontrollable there is in us, urging across glaciers and torrents, and up dangerous heights, let the judgment forbid as it may.

I succeeded in gaining the foot of the cliff on the eastern extremity of the glacier, and there discovered the mouth of a narrow avalanche gully, through which I began to climb, intending to follow it as far as possible, and at least obtain some fine wild views for my pains. Its general course is oblique to the plane of the mountain face, and the metamorphic slates of which the mountain is built are cut by cleavage planes in such a way that they weather off in angular blocks, giving rise to irregular steps that greatly facilitate climbing on the sheer places. I thus made my way into a wilderness of crumbling spires and battlements, built together in bewildering combinations, and glazed in many places with a thin coating of ice, which I had to hammer off with stones. The situation was becoming gradually more perilous; but, having passed several dangerous spots, I dared not think of descending; for, so steep was the entire ascent, one would inevitably fall to the glacier in case a single misstep were made. Knowing, therefore, the tried danger beneath, I became all the more anxious concerning the developments to be made above, and began to be conscious of a vague foreboding of what actually befell; not that I was given to fear, but rather because my instincts, usually so positive and true, seemed vitiated in some way, and were leading me astray. At length, after attaining an elevation of about 12,800 feet, I found myself at the foot of a sheer drop in the bed of the avalanche channel I was tracing, which seemed absolutely to bar further progress. It was only about forty-five or fifty feet high, and somewhat roughened by fissures and projections, but these seemed so slight and insecure as footholds that I tried hard to avoid the precipice altogether by scaling the wall of the channel on either side. But, though less steep, the walls were smoother than the obstructing rock, and repeated efforts only showed that I must either go right ahead or turn back. The tried dangers beneath seemed even greater than that of the cliff in front; therefore, after scanning its face again and again, I began to scale it, picking my holds with intense caution. After gaining a point about halfway to the top, I was suddenly brought to a dead stop, with arms outspread, clinging close to the face of the rock, unable to move hand or foot either up or down. My doom appeared fixed. I must fall. There would be a moment of bewilderment, and then a lifeless rumble down the one general precipice to the glacier below.

When this final danger flashed upon me, I became nerve-shaken for the first time since setting foot on the mountains, and my mind seemed to fill with a stifling smoke. But this terrible eclipse lasted only a moment, when life blazed forth again with preternatural clearness. I seemed suddenly to become possessed of a new sense. The other self, bygone experiences, instinct, or guardian angel— call it what you will—came forward and assumed control. Then my trembling muscles became firm again, every rift and flaw in the rock was seen as through a microscope, and my limbs moved with a positiveness and precision with which I seemed to have nothing at all to do. Had I been borne aloft upon wings, my deliverance could not have been more complete.

Above this memorable spot, the face of the mountain is still more savagely hacked and torn. It is a maze of yawning chasms and gullies, in the angles of which rise beetling crags and piles of detached boulders that seem to have been gotten ready to be launched below. But the strange influx of strength I had received seemed inexhaustible. I found a way without effort, and soon stood upon the topmost crag in the blessed light.

How truly glorious the landscape circled around this noble summit—giant mountains, valleys innumerable, glaciers and meadows, rivers and lakes, with the wide blue sky bent tenderly over them all. But in my first hour of freedom from that terrible shadow, the sunlight in which I was laying seemed all in all.

Looking southward along the axis of the range, the eye is first caught by a row of exceedingly sharp and slender spires, which rise openly to a height of about a thousand feet, above a series of short, residual glaciers that lean back against their bases; their fantastic sculpture and the unrelieved sharpness with which they spring out of the ice rendering them peculiarly wild and striking. These are "The Minarets." Beyond them you behold a sublime wilderness of mountains, their snowy summits towering together in crowded abundance, peak beyond peak, swelling higher, higher as they sweep on southward, until the culminating point of the range is reached on Mount Whitney, near the head of the Kern River, at an elevation of nearly 14,700 feet above the level of the sea.

Westward, the general flank of the range is seen flowing sublimely away from the sharp summits, in smooth undulations; a sea of huge, gray, granite waves dotted with lakes and meadows, and fluted with stupendous canyons that grow steadily deeper as they recede in the distance. Below this gray region lies the dark forest zone, broken here and there by upswelling ridges and domes; and yet beyond lies a yellow, hazy belt, marking the broad plain of the San Joaquin, bounded on its farther side by the blue mountains of the coast.

Turning now to the northward, there in the immediate foreground is the glorious Sierra Crown, with Cathedral Peak, a temple of marvelous architecture, a few degrees to the left of it; the gray, massive form of Mammoth Mountain to the right; while mounts Ord, Gibbs, Dana, Conness, Tower Peak, Castle Peak, Silver Mountain, and a host of noble companions, as yet nameless, make a sublime show along the axis of the range.

Eastward, the whole region seems a land of desolation covered with beautiful light. The torrid volcanic basin of Mono, with its one bare lake fourteen miles long; Owen's Valley and the broad lava table land at its head, dotted with craters, and the massive Inyo Range, rivaling even the Sierra in height; these are spread, map-like, beneath you, with countless ranges beyond, passing and overlapping one another and fading on the glowing horizon.

At a distance of less than three thousand feet below the summit of Mount Ritter you may find tributaries of the San Joaquin and Owen's rivers, bursting forth from the ice and snow of the glaciers that load its flanks; while a little to the north of here are found the highest affluents of the Tuolumne and Merced. Thus, the fountains of four of the principal rivers of California are within a radius of four or five miles.

Lakes are seen gleaming in all sorts of places—round, or oval, or square, like very mirrors; others narrow and sinuous, drawn close around the peaks like silver zones, the highest reflecting only rocks, snow, and the sky. But neither these nor the glaciers, nor the bits of brown meadow and moorland that occur here and there, are large enough to make any marked impression upon the mighty wilderness of mountains. The eye, rejoicing in its freedom, roves about the vast expanse, yet returns again and again to the fountain peaks. Perhaps some one of the multitude excites special attention, some gigantic castle with turret and battlement, or some Gothic cathedral more abundantly spired than Milan's. But, generally, when looking for the first time from an all-embracing standpoint like this, the inexperienced observer is oppressed by the incomprehensible grandeur, variety, and abundance of the mountains rising shoulder to shoulder beyond the reach of vision; and it is only after they have been studied one by one, long and lovingly, that their far-reaching harmonies become manifest. Then, penetrate the wilderness where you may, the main telling features, to which all the surrounding topography is subordinate, are quickly perceived, and the most complicated clusters of peaks stand revealed harmoniously correlated and fashioned like works of art—eloquent monuments of the ancient ice rivers that brought them into relief from the general mass of the range. The canyons, too, some of them a mile deep, mazing wildly through the mighty host of mountains, however lawless and ungovernable at first sight they appear, are at length recognized as the necessary effects of causes which followed each other in harmonious sequence—Nature's poems carved on tables of stone—the simplest and most emphatic of her glacial compositions.

Could we have been here to observe during the glacial period, we should have overlooked a wrinkled ocean of ice as continuous as that now covering the landscapes of Greenland; filling every valley and canyon with only the tops of the fountain peaks rising darkly above the rock-encumbered ice waves like islets in a stormy sea—

those islets the only hints of the glorious landscapes now smiling in the sun. Standing here in the deep, brooding silence all the wilderness seems motionless, as if the work of creation were done. But in the midst of this outer steadfastness we know there is incessant motion and change. Ever and anon, avalanches are falling from yonder peaks. These cliff-bound glaciers, seemingly wedged and immovable, are flowing like water and grinding the rocks beneath them. The lakes are lapping their granite shores and wearing them away, and every one of these rills and young rivers is fretting the air into music, and carrying the mountains to the plains. Here are the roots of all the life of the valleys, and here more simply than elsewhere is the eternal flux of nature manifested. Ice changing to water, lakes to meadows, and mountains to plains. And while we thus contemplate nature's methods of landscape creation, and, reading the records she has carved on the rocks, reconstruct, however imperfectly, the landscapes of the past, we also learn that as these we now behold have succeeded those of the preglacial age, so they in turn are withering and vanishing to be succeeded by others yet unborn.

But in the midst of these fine lessons and landscapes, I had to remember that the sun was wheeling far to the west, while a new way down the mountain had to be discovered to some point on the timber line where I could have a fire; for I had not even burdened myself with a coat. I first scanned the western spurs, hoping some way might appear through which I might reach the northern glacier, and cross its snout; or pass around the lake into which it flows, and thus strike my morning track. This route was soon sufficiently unfolded to show that, if practicable at all, it would require so much time that reaching camp that night would be out of the question. I therefore scrambled back eastward, descending the southern slopes obliquely at the same time. Here the crags seemed less formidable, and the head of a glacier that flows northeast came in sight, which I determined to follow as far as possible, hoping thus to make my way to the foot of the peak on the east side, and thence across the intervening canyons and ridges to camp.

The inclination of the glacier is quite moderate at the head, and, as the sun had softened the névé, I made safe and rapid progress, running and sliding, and keeping up a sharp outlook for crevasses. About half a mile from the head, there is an ice cascade, where the glacier pours over a sharp declivity and is shattered into massive blocks separated by deep, blue fissures. To thread my way through the slippery mazes of this crevassed portion seemed impossible, and I endeavored to avoid it by climbing off to the shoulder of the mountain. But the slopes rapidly steepened and at length fell away in sheer precipices, compelling a return to the ice. Fortunately, the day had been warm enough to loosen the ice crystals so as to admit of hollows being dug in the rotten portions of the blocks, thus enabling me to pick my way with far less difficulty than I had anticipated. Continuing down over the snout, and along the left lateral moraine, was only a confident saunter, showing that the ascent of the mountain by way of this glacier is easy, provided one is armed with an ax to cut steps here and there.

The lower end of the glacier was beautifully waved and barred by the outcropping edges of the bedded ice layers, which represent the annual snowfalls and, to some extent, the irregularities of structure caused by the weathering of the walls of crevasses, and by separate snowfalls which have been followed by rain, hail, thawing and freezing, etc. Small rills were gliding and swirling over the melting surface with a smooth, oily appearance, in channels of pure ice—their quick, compliant movements contrasting most impressively with the rigid, invisible flow of the glacier itself, on whose back they all were riding.

Night drew near before I reached the eastern base of the mountain, and my camp lay many a rugged mile to the north, but ultimate success was assured. It was now only a matter of endurance and ordinary mountain-craft. The sunset was, if possible, yet more beautiful than that of the day before. The Mono landscape seemed to be fairly saturated with warm, purple light. The peaks marshaled along the summit were in shadow, but through every notch and pass streamed vivid sun-fire, soothing and irradiating their rough, black angles, while companies of small, luminous clouds hovered above them like very angels of light.

Darkness came on, but I found my way by the trends of the canyons and the peaks projected against the sky. All excitement died with the light, and then I was weary. But the joyful sound of the waterfall across the lake was heard at last, and soon the stars were seen reflected in the lake itself. Taking my bearings from these, I discovered the little pine thicket in which my nest was, and then I had a rest such as only a tired mountaineer may enjoy. After lying loose and lost for a while, I made a sunrise fire, went down to the lake, dashed water on my head, and dipped a cupful for tea. The revival brought about by bread and tea was as complete as the exhaustion from excessive enjoyment and toil. Then I crept beneath the pine tassels to bed. The wind was frosty and the fire burned low, but my sleep was nonetheless sound, and the evening constellations had swept far to the west before I awoke.

After thawing and resting in the morning sunshine, I saun-tered home—that is, back to the Tuolumne camp—bearing away toward a cluster of peaks that hold the fountain snows of one of the north tributaries of Rush Creek. Here I discovered a group of beautiful glacier lakes, nestled together in a grand amphitheater. Toward evening, I crossed the divide separating the Mono waters from those of the Tuolumne, and entered the glacier basin that now holds the fountain snows of the stream that forms the upper Tuolumne cascades. This stream I traced down through its many dells and gorges, meadows and bogs, reaching the brink of the main Tuolumne at dusk.

A loud whoop for the artists was answered again and again. Their campfire came in sight, and half an hour afterward I was with them. They seemed unreasonably glad to see me. I had been absent only three days; nevertheless, though the weather was fine, they had already been weighing chances as to whether I would ever return, and trying to decide whether they should wait longer or begin to seek their way back to the lowlands. Now their curious troubles were over. They packed their precious sketches, and next morning we set out homeward bound, and in two days entered the Yosemite Valley from the north by way of Indian Canyon.

A Windstorm in the Forest

The mountain winds, like the dew and rain, sunshine and snow, are measured and bestowed with love on the forests to develop their strength and beauty. However restricted the scope of other forest influences, that of the winds is universal. The snow bends and trims the upper forests every winter, the lightning strikes a single tree here and there, while avalanches mow down thousands at a swoop as a gardener trims out a bed of flowers. But the winds go to every tree, fingering every leaf and branch and furrowed bole; not one is forgotten; the mountain pine towering with outstretched arms on the rugged buttresses of the icy peaks, the lowliest and most retiring tenant of the dells; they seek and find them all, caressing them tenderly, bending them in lusty exercise, stimulating their growth, plucking off a leaf or limb as required, or removing an entire tree or grove, now whispering and cooing through the branches like a sleepy child, now roaring like the ocean; the winds blessing the forests, the forests the winds, with ineffable beauty and harmony as the sure result.

After one has seen pines six feet in diameter bending like grasses before a mountain gale, and ever and anon some giant falling with a crash that shakes the hills, it seems astonishing that any, save the lowest thickset trees, could ever have found a period sufficiently stormless to establish themselves; or, once established, that they should not, sooner or later, have been blown down. But when the storm is over, and we behold the same forests tranquil again, towering fresh and unscathed in erect majesty, and consider what centuries of storms have fallen upon them since they were first planted—hail, to break the tender seedlings; lightning, to scorch and shatter; snow, winds, and avalanches, to crush and

overwhelm—while the manifest result of all this wild storm culture is the glorious perfection we behold; then faith in Nature's forestry is established, and we cease to deplore the violence of her most
destructive gales, or of any other storm implement whatsoever.

There are two trees in the Sierra forests that are never blown
down, so long as they continue in sound health. These are the juniper and the dwarf pine of the summit peaks. Their stiff, crooked
roots grip the storm-beaten ledges like eagles' claws, while their
lithe, cord-like branches bend round compliantly, offering but
slight holds for winds, however violent. The other alpine conifers—the needle pine, mountain pine, two-leaved pine, and hemlock spruce—are never thinned out by this agent to any destructive extent, on account of their admirable toughness and the close-
ness of their growth. In general the same is true of the giants of
the lower zones. The kingly sugar pine, towering aloft to a height
of more than two hundred feet, offers a fine mark to storm winds;
but it is not densely foliaged, and its long, horizontal arms swing
'round compliantly in the blast, like tresses of green, fluent algae
in a brook; while the silver firs in most places keep their ranks
well together in united strength. The yellow or silver pine is
more frequently overturned than any other tree on the Sierra,
because its leaves and branches form a larger mass in proportion
to its height, while in many places it is planted sparsely, leaving open lanes through which storms may enter with full force.
Furthermore, because it is distributed along the lower portion of
the range, which was the first to be left bare on the breaking up of
the ice sheet at the close of the glacial winter, the soil it is growing upon has been longer exposed to postglacial weathering, and
consequently is in a more crumbling, decayed condition than the
fresher soils farther up the range, and therefore offers a less secure
anchorage for the roots.

While exploring the forest zones of Mount Shasta, I discovered
the path of a hurricane strewn with thousands of pines of this species. Great and small had been uprooted or wrenched off by sheer
force, making a clean gap, like that made by a snow avalanche. But
hurricanes capable of doing this class of work are rare in the Sierra,
and when we have explored the forests from one extremity of the

range to the other, we are compelled to believe that they are the most beautiful on the face of the earth, however we may regard the agents that have made them so.

There is always something deeply exciting, not only in the sounds of winds in the woods, which exert more or less influence over every mind, but in their varied waterlike flow as manifested by the movements of the trees, especially those of the conifers. By no other trees are they rendered so extensively and impressively visible, not even by the lordly tropic palms or tree ferns responsive to the gentlest breeze. The waving of a forest of the giant sequoias is indescribably impressive and sublime, but the pines seem to me the best interpreters of winds. They are mighty waving goldenrods, ever in tune, singing and writing wind music all their long century lives. Little, however, of this noble tree waving and tree music will you see or hear in the strictly alpine portion of the forests. The burly juniper, whose girth sometimes more than equals its height, is about as rigid as the rocks on which it grows. The slender lash-like sprays of the dwarf pine stream out in wavering ripples, but the tallest and slenderest are far too unyielding to wave even in the heaviest gales. They only shake in quick, short vibrations. The hemlock spruce, however, and the mountain pine, and some of the tallest thickets of the two-leaved species bow in storms with considerable scope and gracefulness. But it is only in the lower and middle zones that the meeting of winds and woods is to be seen in all its grandeur.

One of the most beautiful and exhilarating storms I ever enjoyed in the Sierra occurred in December 1874, when I happened to be exploring one of the tributary valleys of the Yuba River. The sky and the ground and the trees had been thoroughly rain-washed and were dry again. The day was intensely pure, one of those incomparable bits of California winter, warm and balmy and full of white, sparkling sunshine, redolent of all the purest influences of the spring and at the same time enlivened with one of the most bracing windstorms conceivable. Instead of camping out, as I usually do, I then chanced to be stopping at the house of a friend. But when the storm began to sound, I lost no time in pushing out into the woods to enjoy it. For, on such occasions, nature has always something rare to show us, and the danger to life and limb is hardly greater than one would experience crouching deprecatingly beneath a roof.

It was still early morning when I found myself fairly adrift. Delicious sunshine came pouring over the hills, lighting the tops of the pines and setting free a steam of summery fragrance that contrasted strangely with the wild tones of the storm. The air was mottled with pine tassels and bright green plumes that went flashing past in the sunlight like birds pursued. But there was not the slightest dustiness, nothing less pure than leaves, and ripe pollen, and flecks of withered bracken and moss. I heard trees falling for hours at the rate of one every two or three minutes; some uprooted, partly on account of the loose, water-soaked condition of the ground; others broken straight across, where some weakness caused by fire had determined the spot. The gestures of the various trees made a delightful study. Young sugar pines, light and feathery as squirrel tails, were bowing almost to the ground, while the grand old patriarchs, whose massive boles had been tried in a hundred storms, waved solemnly above them, their long, arching branches streaming fluently on the gale, and every needle thrilling and ringing and shedding off keen lances of light like a diamond. The Douglas spruces, with long sprays drawn out in level tresses, and needles massed in a gray, shimmering glow, presented a most striking appearance as they stood in bold relief along the hilltops. The madronos in the dells, with their red bark and large glossy leaves tilted every way, reflected the sunshine in throbbing spangles like those one so often sees on the rippled surface of a glacier lake. But the silver pines were now the most impressively beautiful of all. Colossal spires 200 feet in height waved like supple goldenrods, chanting and bowing low as if in worship, while the whole mass of their long, tremulous foliage was kindled into one continuous blaze of white sun-fire. The force of the gale was such that the most steadfast monarch of them all rocked down to its roots with a motion plainly perceptible when one leaned against it. Nature was holding high festival, and every fiber of the most rigid giants thrilled with glad excitement.

I drifted on through the midst of this passionate music and motion, across many a glen, from ridge to ridge, often halting in the lee of a rock for shelter, or to gaze and listen. Even when the grand anthem had swelled to its highest pitch, I could distinctly hear the varying tones of individual trees, spruce, and fir, and pine, and leafless oak—and even the infinitely gentle rustle of the withered grasses at my feet. Each was expressing itself in its own way—singing its own song and making its own peculiar gestures—manifesting a richness of variety to be found in no other forest I have yet seen. The coniferous woods of Canada, and the Carolinas, and Florida, are made up of trees that resemble one another about as nearly as blades of grass, and grow close together in much the same way. Coniferous trees, in general, seldom possess individual character, such as is manifest among oaks and elms. But the California forests are made up of a greater number of distinct species than any other in the world. And in them we find, not only a marked differentiation into special groups, but also a marked individuality in almost every tree, giving rise to storm effects indescribably glorious.

Toward midday, after a long, tingling scramble through copses of hazel and *Ceanothus,* I gained the summit of the highest ridge in the neighborhood; and then it occurred to me that it would be a fine thing to climb one of the trees to obtain a wider outlook and get my ear close to the Aeolian music of its topmost needles. But under the circumstances, the choice of a tree was a serious matter. One whose instep was not very strong seemed in danger of being blown down, or of being struck by others in case they should fall; another was branchless to a considerable height above the ground, and at the same time too large to be grasped with arms and legs in climbing; while others were not favorably situated for clear views. After cautiously casting about, I made choice of the tallest of a group of Douglas spruces that were growing close together like a tuft of grass, no one of which seemed likely to fall unless all the rest fell with it. Though comparatively young, they were about 100 feet high, and their lithe, brushy tops were rocking and swirling in wild ecstasy. Being accustomed to climb trees in making botanical studies, I experienced no difficulty in reaching the top of this one, and never before did I enjoy so noble an exhilaration of motion. The slender tops fairly flapped and swished in the passionate torrent, bending and swirling backward and forward, round and round, tracing indescribable combinations of vertical and horizontal curves, while I clung with muscles firm braced, like a bobolink on a reed.

In its widest sweeps, my tree-top described an arc of from twenty to thirty degrees, but I felt sure of its elastic temper, having seen others of the same species still more severely tried—bent almost to the ground indeed, in heavy snows without breaking a fiber. I was therefore safe, and free to take the wind into my pulses and enjoy the excited forest from my superb outlook. The view from here must be extremely beautiful in any weather. Now my eye roved over the piney hills and dales as over fields of waving grain, and felt the light running in ripples and broad swelling undulations across the valleys from ridge to ridge, as the shining foliage was stirred by corresponding waves of air. Oftentimes these waves of reflected light would break up suddenly into a kind of beaten foam, and again, after chasing one another in regular order, they would seem to bend forward in concentric curves, and disappear on some hillside, like sea waves on a shelving shore. The quantity of light reflected from the bent needles was so great as to make whole groves appear as if covered with snow, while the black shadows beneath the trees greatly enhanced the effect of the silvery splendor.

Excepting only the shadows, there was nothing somber in all this wild sea of pines. On the contrary, notwithstanding this was the winter season, the colors were remarkably beautiful. The shafts of the pine and *Libocedrus* were brown and purple, and most of the foliage was well tinged with yellow; the laurel groves, with the pale undersides of their leaves turned upward, made masses of gray; and then there was many a dash of chocolate color from clumps of manzanita, and jet of vivid crimson from the bark of the madronos, while the ground on the hillsides, appearing here and there through openings between the groves, displayed masses of pale purple and brown.

The sounds of the storm corresponded gloriously with this wild exuberance of light and motion. The profound bass of the naked branches and boles booming like waterfalls; the quick, tense vibrations of the pine needles, now rising to a shrill, whistling hiss, now falling to a silky murmur; the rustling of laurel groves in the dells, and the keen metallic click of leaf on leaf—all this was heard in easy analysis when the attention was calmly bent.

The varied gestures of the multitude were seen to fine advantage, so that one could recognize the different species at a distance of several miles by this means alone, as well as by their forms and colors, and the way they reflected the light. All seemed strong and comfortable, as if really enjoying the storm, while responding to its most enthusiastic greetings. We hear much nowadays concerning the universal struggle for existence, but no struggle in the common meaning of the word was manifest here; no recognition of danger by any tree; no deprecation; but rather an invincible gladness as remote from exultation as from fear.

I kept my lofty perch for hours, frequently closing my eyes to enjoy the music by itself, or to feast quietly on the delicious fragrance that was streaming past. The fragrance of the woods was less marked than that produced during warm rain, when so many balsamic buds and leaves are steeped like tea; but, from the chafing of resiny branches against each other, and the incessant attrition of myriad needles, the gale was spiced to a very tonic degree. And besides the fragrance from these local sources, there were traces of scents brought from afar. For this wind came first from the sea, rubbing against its fresh, briny waves, then distilled through the redwoods, threading rich ferny gulches, and spreading itself in broad undulating currents over many a flower-enameled ridge of the coast mountains, then across the golden plains, up the purple foothills, and into these piney woods with the varied incense gathered by the way.

Winds are advertisements of all they touch, however much or little we may be able to read them; telling their wanderings even by their scents alone. Mariners detect the flowery perfume of land winds far at sea, and sea winds carry the fragrance of dulse and tangle far inland, where it is quickly recognized, though mingled with the scents of a thousand land flowers. As an illustration of this, I may tell here that I breathed sea air on the Firth of Forth in Scotland, while a boy; then was taken to Wisconsin, where I remained nineteen years; then, without in all this time having breathed one breath of the sea, I walked quietly, alone, from the

middle of the Mississippi Valley to the Gulf of Mexico, on a botanical excursion, and while in Florida, far from the coast, my attention wholly bent on the splendid tropical vegetation about me, I
suddenly recognized a sea breeze, as it came sifting through the
palmettos and blooming vine-tangles, which at once awakened and
set free a thousand dormant associations, and made me a boy again
in Scotland, as if all the intervening years had been annihilated.

Most people like to look at mountain rivers, and bear them in
mind, but few care to look at the winds, though far more beautiful and sublime, and though they become at times about as visible
as flowing water. When the north winds in winter are making
upward sweeps over the curving summits of the High Sierra, the
fact is sometimes published with flying snow-banners a mile long.
Those portions of the winds thus embodied can scarce be wholly
invisible, even to the darkest imagination. And when we look
around over an agitated forest, we may see something of the wind
that stirs it, by its effects upon the trees. Yonder it descends in a
rush of water-like ripples and sweeps over the bending pines from
hill to hill. Nearer, we see detached plumes and leaves, now speed-
ing by on level currents, now whirling in eddies, or, escaping over
the edges of the whirls, soaring aloft on grand, upswelling domes
of air, or tossing on flame-like crests. Smooth, deep currents, cascades, falls, and swirling eddies sing around every tree and leaf, and
over all the varied topography of the region with telling changes
of form, like mountain rivers conforming to the features of their
channels.

After tracing the Sierra streams from their fountains to the
plains, marking where they bloom white in falls, glide in crystal
plumes, surge gray and foam-filled in boulder-choked gorges, and
slip through the woods in long, tranquil reaches after thus learning their language and forms in detail, we may at length hear them
chanting all together in one grand anthem, and comprehend them
all in clear inner vision, covering the range like lace. But even this
spectacle is far less sublime and not a whit more substantial than
what we may behold of these storm-streams of air in the mountain
woods.

We all travel the Milky Way together, trees and men, but it never
occurred to me until this storm day, while swinging in the wind,

that trees are travelers in the ordinary sense. They make many journeys, not extensive ones it is true; but our own little journeys, away and back again, are only little more than tree wavings—many of them not so much.

When the storm began to abate, I dismounted and sauntered down through the calming woods. The storm tones died away, and, turning toward the east, I beheld the countless hosts of the forests hushed and tranquil, towering above one another on the slopes of the hills like a devout audience. The setting sun filled them with amber light and seemed to say, while they listened, "My peace I give unto you."

As I gazed on the impressive scene, all the so-called ruin of the storm was forgotten, and never before did these noble woods appear so fresh, so joyous, so immortal.

Yosemite Falls at Midnight

To Mrs. Ezra S. Carr

MIDNIGHT, YOSEMITE
APRIL 3, 1871

Oh, Mrs. Carr, that you could be here to mingle in this night-noon glory! I am in the upper Yosemite Falls and can hardly calm to write, but from my first baptism hours ago, you have been so present that I must try to fix you a written thought.

In the afternoon I came up the mountain here with a blanket and a piece of bread to spend the night in prayer among the spouts of this fall. But what can I say more than wish again that you might expose your soul to the rays of this heaven?

Silver from the moon illumines this glorious creation which we term "falls," and has laid a magnificent double prismatic bow at its base.

The tissue of the fall is delicately filmed on the outside like the substance of spent clouds, and the stars shine dimly through it. In the solid shafted body of the fall is a vast number of passing caves, black and deep, with close, white, convolving spray for sills and shooting-comet sheaves above and down their sides, like lime crystals in a cave. And every atom of the magnificent being, from the thin, silvery crest that does not dim the stars to the inner arrowy hardened shafts that strike onward like thunderbolts in sound and energy, all is life and spirit: every bolt and spray feels the hand of God. Oh, the music that is blessing me now! The sun of last week has given the grandest notes of all the yearly anthem.

I said that I was going to stop here until morning and pray a whole blessed night with the falls and the moon, but I am too wet and must go down. An hour or two ago I went out somehow on a little seam that extends along the wall behind the falls. I suppose I was in a trance, but I can positively say that I was in the body, for it is sorely battered and wetted. As I was gazing past the thin edge of the fall and away beneath the column to the brow of the rock, some heavy splashes of water struck me, driven hard against the wall. Suddenly I was darkened, down came a section of the outside tissue composed of spent comets. I crouched low, holding my breath, and anchored to some angular flakes of rock, took my baptism with moderately good faith.

When I dared to look up after the swaying column admitted light, I pounced behind a piece of ice and the wall which was wedging tight, and I no longer feared being washed off, and steady moonbeams slanting past the arching meteors gave me confidence to escape to this snug place where McChesney and I slept one night, where I have a fire to dry my socks. This rock shell, extending behind the falls, is about five hundred feet above the base of the fall on the perpendicular rock face.

How little do we know of ourselves, of our profoundest attractions and repulsions, of our spiritual affinities! How interesting does man become considered in his relations to the spirit of this rock and water! How significant does every atom of our world become amid the influences of those beings unseen, spiritual, angelic mountaineers that so throng these pure mansions of crystal foam and purple granite.

I cannot refrain from speaking to this little bush at my side and to the spray drops that come to my paper and to the individual sands of the slopelet I am sitting upon. Ruskin says that the idea of foulness is essentially connected with what he calls dead, unorganized matter. How cordially I disbelieve him tonight, and were he to dwell awhile among the powers of these mountains he would forget all dictionary differences betwixt the clean and the unclean, and he would lose all memory and meaning of the diabolical sin-begotten term foulness.

Well, I must go down. I am disregarding all of the doctors' phys-iology in sitting here in this universal moisture. Farewell to you, and to all the beings about us. I shall have a glorious walk down the mountain in this thin, white light, over the open brows grayed with *Selaginella* and through the thick black shadow caves in the live oaks, all stuck full of snowy lances of moonlight.

[John Muir]

Nut Time in Squirrelville

To Mrs. Ezra S. Carr
Squirrelville, Sequoia Co.
Nut Time

Dear Mrs. Carr:
Do behold the King in his glory, King Sequoia! Behold! Behold! seems all I can say. Some time ago I left all for Sequoia and have been and am at his feet, fasting and praying for light, for is he not the greatest light in the woods, in the world? Where are such columns—of sunshine, tangible, accessible, terrestrialized? Well may I fast, not from bread, but from business, book-making, duty-going, and other trifles, and great is my reward already for the manly, treely sacrifice. What giant truths since coming to Gigantea, what magnificent clusters of Sequoic *becauses*. From here I cannot recite you one, for you are down a thousand fathoms deep in dark political quag, not a burr-length less. But I'm in the woods, woods, woods, and they are in *me-ee-ee*. The King tree and I have sworn eternal love—sworn it without swearing, and I've taken the sacrament with Douglas squirrel, drunk Sequoia wine, Sequoia blood, and with its rosy purple drops I am writing this woody gospel letter.

I never before knew the virtue of Sequoia juice. Seen with sunbeams in it, its color is the most royal of all royal purples. No wonder the Indians instinctively drink it for they know not what. I wish I were so drunk and Sequoical that I could preach the green brown woods to all the juiceless world, descending from this divine wilderness like a John the Baptist, eating Douglas squirrels and wild honey or wild anything, crying, Repent, for the Kingdom of Sequoia is at hand!

There is balm in these leafy Gileads—pungent burrs and living King juice for all defrauded civilization; for sick grangers and politicians; no need of Salt rivers. Sick or successful, come suck Sequoia and be saved.

Douglas squirrel is so pervaded with rosin and burr juice, his flesh can scarce be eaten even by mountaineers. No wonder he is so charged with magnetism! One of the little lions ran across my feet the other day as I lay resting under a fir, and the effect was a thrill like a battery shock. I would eat him no matter how rosiny for the lightning he holds. I wish I could eat wilder things. Think of the grouse with balsam-scented crop stored with spruce buds, the wild sheep full of glacier meadow grass and daisies azure, and the bear burly and brown as Sequoia, eating pine-burrs and wasps' stings and all; then think of the soft lightningless poultice-like pap reeking upon town tables. No wonder cheeks and legs become flabby and fungoid! I wish I were wilder, and so, bless Sequoia, I will be. There is at least a punky spark in my heart and it may blaze in this autumn gold, fanned by the King. Some of my grandfathers must have been born on a muirland for there is heather in me, and tinctures of bog juices, that send me to Cassiope, and oozing through all my veins impel me unhaltingly through endless glacier meadows, seemingly the deeper and danker the better.

See Sequoia aspiring in the upper skies, every summit modeled in fine cycloidal curves as if pressed into unseen molds, every bole warm in the mellow amber sun. How truly godful in mien! I was talking the other day with a duchess and was struck with the grand bow with which she bade me good-bye and thanked me for the glaciers I gave her, but this forenoon King Sequoia bowed to me down in the grove as I stood gazing, and the highbred gestures of the lady seemed rude by contrast.

There goes Squirrel Douglas, the masterspirit of the treetop. It has just occurred to me how his belly is buffy brown, and his back silver gray. Ever since the first Adam of his race saw trees and burrs, his belly has been rubbing upon buff bark, and his back has been combed with silver needles. Would that some of you, wise—

terribly wise—social scientists, might discover some method of living as true to nature as the buff people of the woods, running as free as the winds and waters among the burrs and filbert thickets of these leafy, mothery woods.

The sun is set, and the star candles are being lighted to show me and Douglas squirrel to bed. Therefore, my Carr, good night. You say, "When are you coming down?" Ask the Lord—Lord Sequoia.

[John Muir]

Yosemite Glaciers

YOSEMITE VALLEY, CAL.,
SEPT. 28.

Two years ago, when picking flowers in the mountains back of
Yosemite Valley, I found a book. It was blotted and storm-beaten;
all of its outer pages were mealy and crumbly, the paper seeming
to dissolve like the snow beneath which it had been buried, but
many of the inner pages were well preserved, and though all were
more or less stained and torn, whole chapters were easily readable.
In just this condition is the great open book of Yosemite glaciers
today; its granite pages have been torn and blurred by the same
storms that wasted the castaway book. The grand central chapters of
the Hoffman, and Tenaya, and Nevada glaciers are stained and cor-
roded by the frosts and rains, yet, nevertheless, they contain scarce
one unreadable page; but the outer chapters of the Pohono, and the
Illilouette, and the Yosemite Creek, and Ribbon, and Cascade glaciers are all dimmed and eaten away on the bottom, though the tops
of their pages have not been so long exposed, and still proclaim in
splendid characters the glorious actions of their departed ice. The
glacier which filled the basin of Yosemite Creek was the fourth ice
stream that flowed to Yosemite Valley. It was about fifteen miles in
length by five in breadth at the middle of the main stream, and in
many places was not less than one thousand feet in depth. It united
with the central glaciers in the valley by a mouth reaching from
the east side of El Capitan to Yosemite Point, east of the falls. Its
western rim was rayed with short tributaries, and on the north its
divide from the Tuolumne glacier was deeply grooved; but few if

any of its ridges were here high enough to separate the descending
ice into distinct tributaries. The main central trunk flowed nearly
south, and, at a distance of about ten miles, separated into three
nearly equal branches, which were turned abruptly to the east.

BRANCH BASINS

Those branch basins are laid among the highest spurs of the
Hoffman range, and abound in small, bright lakes, set in the solid
granite without the usual terminal moraine dam. The structure of
those dividing spurs is exactly similar, all three appearing as if ruins
of one mountain, or rather as perfect units hewn from one mountain rock during long ages of glacial activity. As their north sides
are precipitous, and as they extend east and west, they were enabled
to shelter and keep alive their hiding glaciers long after the death
of the main trunk. Their basins are still dazzling bright, and their
lakes have as yet accumulated but narrow rings of border meadow,
because their feeding streams have had but little time to carry the
sand of which they are made. The east bank of the main stream, all
the way from the three forks to the mouth, is a continuous, regular
wall, which also forms the west bank of Indian Canyon glacier
basin. The tributaries of the west side of the main basin touched
the east tributaries of the cascade, and the great Tuolumne glacier
from Mount Dana, the mightiest ice river of this whole region,
flowed past on the north. The declivity of the tributaries was great,
especially those which flowed from the spurs of the Hoffman on
the Tuolumne divide, but the main stream was rather level, and
in approaching Yosemite was compelled to make a considerable
ascent back of Eagle Cliff. To the concentrated currents of the
central glaciers, and to the levelness and width of mouth of this
one, we in a great measure owe the present height of the Yosemite
Falls. Yosemite Creek lives the most tranquil life of all the large
streams that leap into the valley, the others occupying the canyons
of narrower and, consequently, of deeper glaciers, while yet far from
the valley, abound in loud falls and snowy cascades, but Yosemite
Creek flows straight on through smooth meadows and hollows,

with only two or three gentle cascades, and now and then a row
of soothing, rumbling rapids, biding its time, and hoarding up the
best music and poetry of its life for the one anthem at Yosemite, as
planned by the ice.

Yosemite Basin

When a bird's-eye view of Yosemite Basin is obtained from any of
its upper domes, it is seen to possess a great number of dense patches
of black forest, planted in abrupt contact with bare, gray rocks.
Those forest plots mark the number and the size of all the entire
and fragmentary moraines of the basin, as the later eroding agents
have not yet had sufficient time to form a soil fit for the vigorous
life of large trees.

Wherever a deep-wombed tributary was laid against a narrow
ridge, and was also shielded from the sun by compassing rock
shadows, there we invariably find one or more small terminal
moraines, because when such tributaries were melted off from the
trunk they retired to those upper strongholds of shade, and lived
and worked in full independence, and the moraines which they
built are left entire because the water-collecting basins behind
them are too small to make streams large enough to wash them
away; but in the basins of exposed tributaries there are no terminal
moraines, because their glaciers died *with* the trunk. Medial and
lateral moraines are common upon all the outside slopes, some of
them nearly perfect in form; but down in the main basin there is
not left one unaltered moraine of any kind, immense floods having
washed down and leveled them into border meadows for the present stream, and into sandy flower beds and fields for forests.

Glacier History

Such was Yosemite glacier, and such is its basin, the magnificent
work of its hands. There is sublimity in the life of a glacier. Water
rivers work openly, and so do the rains and the gentle dews, and the
great sea also grasping all the world; and even this universal ocean

of breath, though invisible, yet speaks aloud in a thousand voices and proclaims its modes of working and its power; but glaciers work apart from men, exerting their tremendous energies in silence and darkness, outspread, spirit-like, brooding above pre-destined rocks unknown to light, unborn, working on unwearied through unmeasured times, unhalting as the stars, until at length, their creations complete, their mountains brought forth, homes made for the meadows and the lakes, moraine banks for chosen flowers, and fields for waiting forests, earnest, calm as when they came in crystals from the sky, they depart.

The great valley itself, together with all of its various domes and walls, was brought forth and fashioned by a grand combination of glaciers, acting in certain directions against granite of peculiar physical structure. All of the rocks and mountains and lakes and meadows of the whole upper Merced basin received their specific forms and carvings almost entirely from this same agency of ice.

I have been drifting about among the rocks of this region for several years, anxious to spell out some of the mountain truths which are written here; and since the number, and magnitude, and significance of these ice rivers began to appear, I have become anxious for more exact knowledge regarding them; with this object, supplying myself with blankets and bread, I climbed out of Yosemite by Indian Canyon, and am now searching the upper rocks and moraines for readable glacier manuscript.

I meant to begin by exploring the main trunk glacier of Yosemite Creek, together with all of its rim tributaries one by one, gathering what data I could find regarding their depth, direction of flow, the kind and amount of work which each had done, etc., but when I was upon the El Capitan Mountain, seeking for the western shore of the main stream, I discovered that the Yosemite Creek glacier was not the lowest ice stream which flowed to the valley, but that the Ribbon Stream basin west of El Capitan had also been occupied by a glacier, which flowed nearly south, and united with the main central glaciers of the summits in the valley below El Capitan.

RIBBON STREAM BASIN

I spent two days in this new basin. It must have been one of the smallest ice streams that entered the valley being only about four miles in length by three in width. It received some small tributaries from the slopes of El Capitan ridge, which flowed south 35° west; but most of its ice was derived from a spur of the Hoffman group, running nearly southwest. The slope of its bed is steep and pretty regular, and it must have flowed with considerable velocity. I have not thus far discovered any of the original striated surfaces, though possibly some patches may still exist somewhere in the basin upon hard plates of quartz, or where a boulder of protecting form has settled upon a rounded surface. I found many such patches in the basin of Yosemite Glacier; one within half a mile of the top of the falls—about two feet square in extent of surface, very perfect in polish, and its striae distinct, although the surrounding unprotected rock is disintegrated to a depth of at least four inches. As this small glacier sloped fully with unsheltered bosom to the sun, it was one of the first to die, and of course its tablets have been longer exposed to blurring rains and dews, and all eroding agents; but notwithstanding the countless blotting, crumbling storms which have fallen upon the historic lithographs of its surface, the great truth of its former existence, printed in characters of moraine and meadow and valley groove, is still as clear as when every one of its pebbles and newborn rocks gleamed forth the full unshadowed poetry of its whole life. With the exception of a few castled piles and broken domes upon its east banks, its basin is rather smooth and lake-like, but it has charming meadows, most interesting in their present flora and glacier history, and noble forests of the two silver firs (*Picea amabilis* and *P. grandis*) planted upon moraines spread out and leveled by overflowing waters.

These researches in the basin of the Ribbon Creek recalled some observations made by me some time ago in the lower portions of the basins of the Cascade and Tamarac streams, and I now thought it probable that careful search would discover abundant traces of glacial action in those basins also. Accordingly, on reaching the

highest northern slope of the Ribbon, I obtained comprehensive
views of both the Cascade and Tamarac basins, and amid their
countless adornments could note many forms of lake and rock
which appeared as genuine glacier characters unmarred and unaltered. Running down the bare slope of an icy-looking canyon, in
less than half an hour I came upon a large patch of the old glacier
bed, polished and striated, with the direction of the flow of the
long dead stream clearly written—South 40° West. This proved
to be the lowest, easternmost tributary of the Cascade glacier. I
proceeded westward as far as the Cascade meadows on the Mono
trail, then turning to the right, entered the mouth of the tributary
at the head of the meadows. Here there is a well-defined terminal
moraine, and the ends of both ridges which formed the banks of
the ice are broken and precipitous, giving evidence of great pressure. I followed up this tributary to its source on the west bank of
the Yosemite glacier about two miles north of the Mono trail, and
throughout its entire length there is abundance of polished tablets
with moraines, rock sculpture, etc., giving glacier testimony as
clear and indisputable as can be found in the most recent glacier
pathways of the Alps.

Vanished Glaciers

I would gladly have explored the main trunk of this beautiful
basin, from its highest snows upon the divide of the Tuolumne, to
its mouth in the Merced Canyon below Yosemite, but alas! I had
not sufficient bread; besides, I felt sure that I should also have to
explore the Tamarac basin, and, following westward among the
fainter, most changed, and covered glacier pathways, I might probably be called as far as the end of the Pilot Peak Ridge. Therefore,
I concluded to leave those lower chapters for future lessons, and go
on with the easier Yosemite pages which I had already begun.

But before taking leave of those lower streams let me distinctly
state that in my opinion future investigation will discover proofs
of the existence in the earlier ages of Sierra Nevada ice, of vast glaciers which flowed to the very foot of the range. Already it is clear
that all of the upper basins were filled with ice so deep and universal
that but few of the highest crests and ridges were sufficiently great to

separate it into individual glaciers, many of the highest mountains having been flowed over and rounded like the boulders in a river. Glaciers poured into Yosemite by every one of its canyons, and at a comparatively recent period of its history, its northern wall, with perhaps the single exception of the crest of Eagle Cliff, was covered by one unbroken flow of ice, the several glaciers having united before they reached the wall.

SEPTEMBER 30—Last evening I was camped in a small round glacier meadow, at the head of the easternmost tributary of the cascade. The meadow was velvet with grass, and circled with the most beautiful of all the conifers, the Williamson spruce. I built a great fire, and the daisies of the sod rayed as if conscious of a sun. As I lay on my back, feeling the presence of the trees—gleaming upon the dark, and gushing with life—coming closer and closer about me, and saw the small round sky coming down with its stars to dome my trees, I said, "Never was mountain mansion more beautiful, more spiritual, never was mortal wanderer more blessedly homed." When the sun rose, my charmed walls were taken down, the trees returned to the common fund of the forest, and my little sky fused back into the measureless blue, I was left upon common ground to follow my glacier labor.

YOSEMITE RIVER BASINS

I followed the main Yosemite River northward, passing round the head of the second Yosemite tributary, which flowed about northeast until bent southward by the main current. About noon, I came to the basin of the third ice tributary of the west rim, a place of domes which had long engaged my attention, and as I was anxious to study their structure, and the various moraines, etc., of the little glacier which had issued from their midst, I camped here close to the foot of two of the most beautiful of the domes, in a sheltered hollow, the womb of the glacier. At the foot of these two domes are two lakes exactly alike in size and history, beautiful as any I ever beheld; first there is the crystal water center, then a yellowish fringe of *Carex*, which has long arching leaves that dip into the water, then a beveled bossy border of yellow *Sphagnum* moss, exactly marking the limits of the lake, farther back is a narrow zone of dryer meadow, smooth and purple with grasses which grow in soft plushy sods, interrupted here and there by clumpy gatherings of blue berry bushes. The purple *Kalmia* grows here also, and the splendidly flowered *Phyllodoce,* but these are small and weave into the sod, spreading low in the grasses and glowing with them. Beside these flowering shrubs, the meadow is lightly sprinkled with daisies and *Dodecatheons* and white violets, most lovely meadows divinely adjusted to most lovely lakes.

In the afternoon I followed down the bed of the tributary to its junction with the main glacier; then, turning to the right, crossed the mouths of the first two tributaries, which I had passed in the morning; then, bearing east, examined a cross section of the main trunk, and reached camp by following up the north bank of the tributary. Between the three tributaries above-mentioned are well defined medial moraines, having been preserved from leveling floods by their position on the higher slopes, with but small water-collecting basins behind them. Down at their junctions, where they were swept round by the main stream, is a large, level field of moraine matter, which, like all the drift fields of this basin, is plant-ed with heavy forests, composed mainly of a pine and fir (*Pinus contorta,* and *Picea amabilis*). This forest is now on fire. I wanted to pass through it, but feared the falling trees. As I stood watching the flapping flames and estimating chances, a tall blazing pine crashed across the gap which I wished to pass, and in a few minutes two more fell. This stirred a broken thought about special providences, and caused me to go around out of danger. *Pinus contorta* is very susceptible of fire, as it grows very close, in grovy thickets, and usually every tree is trickled and beaded with gum. The summit forests are almost entirely composed of this pine.

DEER IN THE VALLEY

Emerging from this wooded moraine I found a great quantity of loose separate boulders upon a polished hilltop, which had formed a part of the bottom of the main ice stream. They were of extraordinary size, some large as houses, and I started northward to seek the mountain from which they had been torn. I had gone but a little way when I discovered a deer quietly feeding upon a narrow strip of green meadow about sixty or seventy yards ahead of me. As the wind blew gently toward it, I thought the opportunity good for testing the truth of hunters' accounts of the deer's wonderful keenness of scent, and stood quite still, and as the deer continued to feed tranquilly, only casting round his head upon his shoulder occasionally to drive away the flies, I began to think that his nose was no better than my own, when suddenly, as if pierced by a bullet, he sprang up into the air and galloped confusedly off without turning to look; but in a few seconds, as if doubtful of the direction of the danger, he came bounding back, caught a glimpse of me, and ran off a second time in a settled direction.

The Yosemite basin is a favorite summer home of the deer. The leguminous vines and juicy grasses of the great moraines supply savory food, while the many high hidings of the Hoffman Mountains, accessible by narrow passes, afford favorite shelter. Grizzly and brown bears also love Yosemite Creek. Berries of the dwarf manzanita, and acorns of the dwarf live oak are abundant upon the dry hilltops; and these with some plants, and the larvae of black ants, are the favorite food of bears, if varied occasionally by a stolen sheep or a shepherd. The gorges of the Tuolumne Canyon, on the north end of the basin, are their principal hiding places in this region. Higher in the range their food is not plentiful, and lower they are molested by man.

On returning to camp I passed three of the domes of the north bank, and was struck with the exact similarity of their structure, the same concentric layers, with a perpendicular cleavage also, but less perfectly developed and more irregular. This little dome tributary, about two-and-a-half miles long by one-and-a-half wide, must have been one of the most beautiful of the basin; all of its upper circling rim is adorned with domes, some half born, sunk in the parent rock; some broken and torn upon the sides by the ice, and a few nearly perfect, from their greater strength of structure or more favorable position. The two lakes above described are the only ones of the tributary basin, both domes and lakes handiwork of the glacier.

A Glacier's Death

In the waning days of this mountain ice, when the main river began to shallow and break like a summer cloud, its crests and domes rising higher and higher, and island rocks coming to light far out in the main current, then many a tributary died, and this one, cut off from its trunk, moved slowly back amid the gurgling and gushing of its bleeding rills, until, crouching in the shadows of this half-mile hollow, it lived a feeble separate life. Here its days come and go, and the hiding glacier lives and works. It brings boulders and sand and fine dust polishings from its sheltering domes and canyons, building up a terminal moraine, which forms a dam for the waters which issue from it; and beneath, working in the dark, it scoops a shallow lake basin. Again the glacier retires, crouching under cooler shadows, and a cluster of steady years enables the dying glacier to make yet another moraine dam like the first; and, where the granite begins to rise in curves to form the upper dam, it scoops another lake. Its last work is done, and it dies. The twin lakes are full of pure green water, and floating masses of snow and broken ice. The domes, perfect in sculpture, gleam in newborn purity, lakes and domes reflecting each other bright as the ice which made them. God's seasons circle on, glad brooks born of the snow and the rain sing in the rocks, and carry sand to the naked lakes, and, in the fullness of time comes many a chosen plant; first a lowly *Carex* with dark brown spikes, then taller sedges and rushes, fixing a shallow soil, and now come many grasses, and daisies, and blooming shrubs, until lake and meadow growing throughout the season like a flower in summer, develop to the perfect beauty of today.

How softly comes night to the mountains. Shadows grow upon all the landscape; only the Hoffman Peaks are open to the sun. Down in this hollow it is twilight, and my two domes, more impressive than in broad day, seem to approach me. They are not vast and over-spiritual, like Yosemite Tissiack, but comprehensible and companionable, and susceptible of human affinities. The darkness grows, and all of their finer sculpture dims. Now the great arches and deep curves sink also, and the whole structure is massed in black against the starry sky.

I have set fire to two pine logs, and the neighboring trees are coming to my charmed circle of light. The two-leaved pine, with sprays and tassels innumerable, the silver fir, with magnificent frouded whorls of shining boughs, and the graceful nodding spruce, dripping with cones, and seeming yet more spiritual in this campfire light. Grandly do my logs give back their light, slow gleaned from suns of a hundred summers, garnered beautifully away in dotted cells and in beads of amber gum; and, together with this outgush of light, seems to flow all the other riches of their life, and their living companions are looking down as if to witness their perfect and beautiful death. But I am weary and must rest. Good night to my two logs and two lakes, and to my two domes high and black on the sky, with a cluster of stars between.

PART FOUR:

The Global Adventurer

Eskimos and Walrus

STEAMER CORWIN, PLOVER BAY, JUNE 15, 1881.

We left our anchorage in St. Lawrence Bay at four in the morning, June 7, and steered once more for Plover Bay. The norther that had been blowing so long gave place to a light southerly breeze, and a gentle dusting of snow was falling. In the afternoon the sea became smooth and glassy as a mountain lake, and the clouds lifted, gradually unveiling the Siberian coast up to the tops of the mountains. First the black bluffs, standing close to the water, came in sight; then the white slopes, and then one summit after another until a continuous range forty or fifty miles long could be seen from one point of view, forming a very beautiful landscape. Smooth, dull, dark water in the foreground; next, a broad belt of ice mostly white like snow, with numerous masses of blue and black shade among its jagged, uplifted blocks. Then a strip of comparatively low shore, black and gray; and back of that the pure white mountains, with only here and there dark spots, where the rock faces are too steep for snow to lie upon. Sharp peaks were seen, fluted by avalanches; glacier wombs, delicate in curve and outline as shells; rounded, overswept brows and domes, and long, withdrawing valleys leading back into the highest alpine groups, whence flowed noble glaciers in imposing ranks into what is now Bering Sea.

We had hoped the gale had broken and driven away the floe that barred our way on the fifth [of June], but while yet thirty miles from the entrance of the bay we were again stopped by an immense field of heavy ice that stretched from the shore southeastward as far as the eye could reach. We pushed slowly into the edge of it a few miles, looking for some opening, but the man in the crow's nest reported it all solid ahead and no water in sight. We thereupon steamed out and steered across to St. Lawrence Island to bide our time.

While sailing amid the loose blocks of ice that form the edge of the pack, we saw a walrus, and soon afterward a second one with its young. The captain shot and killed the mother from the pilot-house, and the dinghy was lowered to tow it alongside. The eyes of our Indian passengers sparkled with delight in expectation of good meat after enduring poor fare aboard the ship. After floating for eight or ten minutes, she sank to the bottom and was lost—a sad fate and a luckless deed.

It was pitiful to see the young one swimming around its dying mother, heeding neither the ship nor the boat. They are said to be very affectionate and bold in the defense of one another against every enemy whatever. We have as yet seen but few, though in some places they are found in countless thousands. Many vessels are exclusively employed in killing them on the eastern Greenland coast, and along some portions of the coast of Asia. Here also, the whalers, when they have poor success in whaling, devote them-selves to walrus hunting, both for the oil they yield and for the valuable ivory. The latter is worth from forty to seventy cents per pound in San Francisco, and a pair of large tusks weighs from eight to ten pounds.

Along all the coasts, both of Asia and of America, the natives hunt and kill this animal, which to them is hardly less important for food and other uses than the seals. A large walrus is said to weigh from one to two tons. Its tough hide is used for cordage, and to cover canoes. The flesh is excellent, while the ivory formerly was employed for spear heads and other uses, and is now an important article of trade for guns, ammunition, calico, bread, flour, molas-ses, etc. The natives now kill a good many whales, having obtained lances and harpoons from the whites. Bone, in good years, is more important than the ivory, and furs are traded, also, in considerable quantity. By all these means they obtain more of the white man's goods than is well used. They probably were better off before they were possessed of a single civilized blessing—so many are the evils accompanying them!

Our Chukchi passenger does not appear to entertain a very good opinion of the St. Lawrence natives. He advised the captain to keep a close watch of those he allowed to come aboard. We asked him today the Chukchi name of ice, which he gave as "eigleegle." When we said that another of his people called it "tingting," he replied that that was the way poor common people spoke the word, but that rich people, the upper aristocratic class to which he belonged, called it "eigleegle." His father, being a rich man, had three wives; most of his tribe, he said, have only one.

At nine o'clock in the evening we were still more than an hour's run from St. Lawrence Island, though according to reckoning we should have reached the northeast end of the island at eight o'clock. We had been carried north about sixteen miles, since leaving St. Lawrence Bay, by the current setting through the strait. The water, having been driven south by the north gale, was pouring north with greater velocity than ordinary. The sky was a mass of dark, grainless cloud, banded slightly near the northwest horizon; one band, a degree in breadth above the sun, was deep indigo, with a few short streaks of orange and red. We have not seen a star since leaving San Francisco, and have seen the sun perfectly cloudless only once! We came to anchor near the northwest end of the island about midnight.

The next day, the eighth of June, was calm and mild. A canoe with ten men and women came alongside this morning, just arrived from Plover Bay, on their way home. They made signs of weariness, having pulled hard against this heavy current. The distance is fifty miles. It is not easy to understand how they manage to find their way in thick weather, when it is difficult enough for seamen with charts and compass.

In trying to account for the observed similarity between the peoples of the opposite shores of Asia and America, and the faunas and floras, scientists have long been combating a difficulty that does not exist save in their own minds. They have suggested that canoes and ships from both shores either were wrecked and drifted from one to the other, or that natives crossed on the ice which every year fills Bering Strait. As today, so from time immemorial canoes have crossed for trade or mere pleasure, steering by the swell of the sea when out of sight of land. As to crossing on the ice, the natives tell me that they frequently go with their dogsleds from the Siberian side to the Diomedes, those halfway houses along the route, but seldom or never from the Diomedes to the American side, on account of the movements of the ice. But, though both means of communication, assumed to account for distribution as it is found to exist today, were left out, land communication in any case undoubtedly existed, just previous to the glacial period, as far south as the Aleutian Islands, and northward beyond the mouth of the strait.

While groping in the dense fogs that hang over this region, sailors find their way at times by the flight of the innumerable seabirds that come and go from the sea to the shore. The direction, at least, of the land is indicated, which is very important in the case of small islands. How the birds find their way is a mystery.

This canoe alongside was "two sleeps" in making the passage. Time, I suppose, is reckoned by sleeps during summer, as there is no night and only one day. They at once began to trade eagerly, seeming to fear that they would be left unvisited, now that the whalers have all gone to the Arctic. In the forenoon, after the natives had left, we took advantage of the calm weather to go in search of the wrecked *Lolita*, which went ashore last fall a few miles to the north of here. On the way we passed through a good deal of ice in flat cakes that had been formed in a deep still bay, sheltered from floating ice which jams and packs it. This ice did not seem to be more than two or three feet thick, possibly the depth to which it froze last winter less the amount melted and evaporated since spring commenced.

Walruses, in groups numbering from two to fifty, were lying on cakes of ice. They were too shy, however, to be approached within shooting range, though many attempts were made. Some of the animals were as bulky, apparently, as oxen. They would awaken at the sound of the vessel crunching through the loose ice, lift their heads and rear as high as possible, then drop or plunge into the water. The ponderous fellows took headers in large groups; twenty pairs of flippers sometimes were in the air at once. They can stay under water five or six minutes, then come up to blow. If they are near the ship they dive again instantly, going down like porpoises, always exposing a large curving mass of their body while dropping their heads, and, lastly, their flippers are stretched aloft for an instant. Sometimes they show fight, make combined attacks on boats, and defend one another bravely. The cakes on which they congregate are of course very dirty, and show to a great distance. Since they soon sink when killed in the water, they are hunted mostly on the ice, and, when it is rough and hummocky, are easily approached.

We were not successful in finding the *Lolita*, so we steamed back to our anchorage in the lee of a high bluff near the Eskimo village. Soon three or four canoes came alongside, loaded with furs, ivory, and whalebone. Molasses, which they carry away in bladders and seal skins, is with them a favorite article of trade. Mixed with flour and blocks of "black skin," it is esteemed, by Eskimo palates, a dish fit for the gods. A group of listeners laughed heartily when I described a mixture that I thought would be to their taste. They smacked their lips, and shouted, "Yes! Yes!" One brought as a present to our Chukchi, the reindeer man's son, a chunk of "black skin" that, in color and odor, seemed to be more than a year old. He, no doubt, judged that our Chukchi, if not starving, was at least faring poorly on civilized trash.

A study of the different Eskimo faces, while important trades were pending, was very interesting. They are better behaved than white men, not half so greedy, shameless, or dishonest. I made a few sketches of marked faces. One, who received a fathom of calico more than was agreed upon, seemed extravagantly delighted and grateful. He was lost in admiration of the captain, whose hand he shook heartily.

We continued at anchor here the following day, June 9. It was snowing and the decks were sloppy. Several canoe loads of Eskimos came aboard, and there was a brisk trade in furs, mostly reindeer hides and parkas for winter use; also fox [skins] and some whalebone and walrus ivory. Flour and molasses were the articles most in demand. Some of the women, heedless of the weather, brought their boys, girls, and babies. One little thing that the proud mother held up for our admiration smiled delightfully, exposing her two precious new teeth. No happier baby could be found in warm parlors, where loving attendants anticipate every want and the looms of the world afford their best in the way of soft fabrics. She looked gaily out at the strange colors about her from her bit of a fur bag, and when she fell asleep, her mother laid her upon three oars that were set side by side across the canoe. The snowflakes fell on her face, yet she slept soundly for hours while I watched her, and she never cried. All the youngsters had to be furnished with a little bread which both fathers and mothers begged for them, saying, "He *little* fellow, *little* fellow."

Four walrus heads were brought aboard and the ivory sold, while the natives, men and women, sat down to dine on them with butcher knives. They cut off the flesh and ate it raw, apparently with good relish. As usual, each mouthful was cut off while held between the teeth. To our surprise they never cut themselves. They seemed to enjoy selecting tidbits from different parts of the head, turning it over frequently and examining pieces here and there, like a family leisurely finishing the wrecked hull of a last day's dinner turkey.

These people interest me greatly, and it is worth coming far to know them, however slightly. The smile, or, rather, broad grin of that Eskimo baby went directly to my heart, and I shall remember it as long as I live. When its features had subsided into perfect repose, the laugh gone from its dark eyes, and the lips closed over its two teeth, I could make its sweet smile bloom out again as often as I nodded and chirruped to it. Heaven bless it! Some of the boys, too, lads from eight to twelve years of age, were well behaved, bashful, and usually laughed and turned away their faces when looked at. But there was a response in their eyes which made you feel that they are your very brothers.

Stickeen vs. the Glacier

Stickeen seemed able for anything. Doubtless we could have weathered the storm for one night, dancing on a flat spot to keep from freezing, and I faced the threat without feeling anything like despair; but we were hungry and wet, and the wind from the mountains was still thick with snow and bitterly cold, so of course that night would have seemed a very long one. I could not see far enough through the blurring snow to judge in which general direction the least dangerous route lay, while the few dim, momentary glimpses I caught of mountains through rifts in the flying clouds were far from encouraging either as weather signs or as guides. I had simply to grope my way from crevasse to crevasse, holding a general direction by the ice structure, which was not to be seen everywhere, and partly by the wind. Again and again I was put to my mettle, but Stickeen followed easily, his nerve apparently growing more unflinching as the danger increased. So it always is with mountaineers when hard beset. Running hard and jumping, holding every minute of the remaining daylight, poor as it was, precious, we doggedly persevered and tried to hope that every difficult crevasse we overcame would prove to be the last of its kind. But on the contrary, as we advanced they became more deadly trying.

At length our way was barred by a very wide and straight crevasse, which I traced rapidly northward a mile or so without finding a crossing or hope of one; then down the glacier about as far, to where it united with another uncrossable crevasse. In all this distance of perhaps two miles there was only one place where I could possibly jump it, but the width of this jump was the utmost I dared attempt, while the danger of slipping on the farther side was so great that I was loath to try it. Furthermore, the side I was on was about a foot higher than the other, and even with this advantage the crevasse seemed dangerously wide. One is liable to underestimate the width of crevasses where the magnitudes in general are great. I therefore stared at this one mighty keenly, estimating its width and the shape of the edge on the farther side, until I thought that I could jump it if necessary, but that in case I should be compelled to jump back from the lower side I might fail. Now, a cautious mountaineer seldom takes a step on unknown ground which seems at all dangerous that he cannot retrace in case he should be stopped by unseen obstacles ahead. This is the rule of mountaineers who live long, and, though in haste, I compelled myself to sit down and calmly deliberate before I broke it.

Retracing my devious path in imagination as if it were drawn on a chart, I saw that I was recrossing the glacier a mile or two farther upstream than the course pursued in the morning, and that I was now entangled in a section I had not before seen. Should I risk this dangerous jump, or try to regain the woods on the west shore, make a fire, and have only hunger to endure while waiting for a new day? I had already crossed so broad a stretch of dangerous ice that I saw it would be difficult to get back to the woods through the storm before dark, and the attempt would most likely result in a dismal night-dance on the glacier; while just beyond the present barrier the surface seemed more promising, and the east shore was now perhaps about as near as the west. I was therefore eager to go on. But this wide jump was a dreadful obstacle.

At length, because of the dangers already behind me, I determined to venture against those that might be ahead, jumped and landed well, but with so little to spare that I more than ever dreaded being compelled to take that jump back from the lower side. Stickeen followed, making nothing of it, and we ran eagerly forward, hoping we were leaving all our troubles behind. But within the distance of a few hundred yards we were stopped by the widest crevasse yet encountered. Of course I made haste to explore it, hoping all might yet be remedied by finding a bridge or a way around either end. About three-fourths of a mile upstream I found that it united with the one we had just crossed, as I feared it would. Then, tracing it down, I found it joined the same crevasse at the lower end also, maintaining throughout its whole course a width of forty to fifty feet. Thus to my dismay I discovered that we were on a narrow island about two miles long, with two barely possible ways of escape: one back by the way we came, the other ahead by an almost inaccessible sliver-bridge that crossed the great crevasse from near the middle of it!

After this nerve-trying discovery I ran back to the sliver-bridge and cautiously examined it. Crevasses, caused by strains from variations in the rate of motion of different parts of the glacier and convexities in the channel, are mere cracks when they first open, so narrow as hardly to admit the blade of a pocketknife, and gradually widen according to the extent of the strain and the depth of the glacier. Now some of these cracks are interrupted, like the cracks in wood, and in opening, the strip of ice between overlapping ends is dragged out and may maintain a continuous connection between the sides, just as the two sides of a slivered crack in wood that is being split are connected. Some crevasses remain open for months or even years, and by the melting of their sides continue to increase in width long after the opening strain has ceased; while the sliver-bridges, level on top at first and perfectly safe, are at length melted to thin, vertical, knife-edged blades, the upper portion being most exposed to the weather; and since the exposure is greatest in the middle, they at length curve downward like the cables of suspension bridges. This one was evidently very old, for it had been weathered and wasted until it was the most dangerous and inaccessible that ever lay in my way. The width of the crevasse was here about fifty feet, and the sliver crossing diagonally was about seventy feet long; its thin knife-edge near the middle was depressed twenty-five or thirty feet below the level of the glacier, and the upcurving ends were attached to the sides eight or ten feet below the brink. Getting down the nearly vertical wall to the end of the sliver and up the other side were the main difficulties, and they seemed all but insurmountable. Of the many perils encountered in my years of wandering on mountains and glaciers none seemed so plain and stern and merciless as this. And it was presented when we were wet to the skin and hungry, the sky dark with quick driving snow, and the night near. But we were forced to face it. It was a tremendous necessity.

Beginning, not immediately above the sunken end of the bridge, but a little to one side, I cut a deep hollow on the brink for my knees to rest in. Then, leaning over, with my short-handled ax, I cut a step sixteen or eighteen inches below, which on account of the sheerness of the wall was necessarily shallow. That step, however, was well made; its floor sloped slightly inward and formed a good hold for my heels. Then, slipping cautiously upon it, and crouching as low as possible, with my left side toward the wall I steadied myself against the wind with my left hand in a slight notch, while with the right I cut other similar steps and notches in succession, guarding against losing balance by glinting of the ax, or by wind gusts, for life and death were in every stroke and in the niceness of finish of every foothold.

After the end of the bridge was reached I chipped it down until I had made a level platform six or eight inches wide, and it was a trying thing to poise on this little slippery platform while bending over to get safely astride of the sliver. Crossing was then comparatively easy by chipping off the sharp edge with short, careful strokes, and hitching forward an inch or two at a time, keeping my balance with my knees pressed against the sides. The tremendous abyss on either hand I studiously ignored. To me the edge of that blue sliver was then all the world. But the most trying part of the adventure, after working my way across inch by inch and chipping another small platform, was to rise from the safe position astride and to cut a stepladder in the nearly vertical face of the wall— chipping, climbing, holding on with feet and fingers in mere notches. At such times one's whole body is eye, and common skill and fortitude are replaced by power beyond our call or knowledge. Never before had I been so long under deadly strain. How I got up that cliff I could never tell. The thing seemed to have been done by somebody else. I never have held death in contempt, though in the course of my explorations I have oftentimes felt that to meet one's fate on a noble mountain, or in the heart of a glacier, would be blessed as compared with death from disease, or from some shabby lowland accident. But the best death, quick and crystal-pure, set so glaringly open before us, is hard enough to face, even though we feel gratefully sure that we have already had happiness enough for a dozen lives.

But poor Stickeen, the wee, hairy, sleekit beastie, think of him! When I had decided to dare the bridge, and while I was on my knees chipping a hollow on the rounded brow above it, he came behind me, pushed his head past my shoulder, looked down and across, scanned the sliver and its approaches with his mysterious eyes, then looked me in the face with a startled air of surprise and concern, and began to mutter and whine, saying as plainly as if speaking with words, "Surely, you are not going into that awful place." This was the first time I had seen him gaze deliberately into a crevasse, or into my face with an eager, speaking, troubled look. That he should have recognized and appreciated the danger at the first glance showed wonderful sagacity. Never before had the daring midget seemed to know that ice was slippery or that there was any such thing as danger anywhere. His looks and tones of voice when he began to complain and speak his fears were so human that I unconsciously talked to him in sympathy as I would to a frightened boy, and in trying to calm his fears perhaps in some measure moderated my own. "Hush your fears, my boy," I said, "we will get across safe, though it is not going to be easy. No right way is easy in this rough world. We must risk our lives to save them. At the worst we can only slip, and then how grand a grave we will have, and by and by our nice bones will do good in the terminal moraine."

But my sermon was far from reassuring him: he began to cry, and after taking another piercing look at the tremendous gulf, ran away in desperate excitement, seeking some other crossing. By the time he got back, baffled of course, I had made a step or two. I dared not look back, but he made himself heard, and when he saw that I was certainly bent on crossing he cried aloud in despair. The danger was enough to daunt anybody, but it seems wonderful that he should have been able to weigh and appreciate it so justly. No mountaineer could have seen it more quickly or judged it more wisely, discriminating between real and apparent peril.

When I gained the other side, he screamed louder than ever, and after running back and forth in vain search for a way of escape, he would return to the brink of the crevasse above the bridge, moaning and wailing as if in the bitterness of death. Could this be the silent, philosophic Stickeen? I shouted encouragement, telling him the bridge was not as bad as it looked, that I had left it flat and safe for his feet, and he could walk it easily. But he was afraid to try. Strange so small an animal should be capable of such big, wise fears. I called again and again in a reassuring tone to come on and fear nothing; that he could come if he would only try. He would hush for a moment, look down again at the bridge, and shout his unshakable conviction that he could never, never come that way; then lie back in despair, as if howling, "O-o-oh! What a place! No-o-o, I can never go-o-o down there!" His natural composure and courage had vanished utterly in a tumultuous storm of fear. Had the danger been less, his distress would have seemed ridiculous. But in this dismal, merciless abyss lay the shadow of death, and his heartrending cries might well have called Heaven to his help. Perhaps they did. So hidden before, he was now transparent, and one could see the workings of his heart and mind like the movements of a clock out of its case. His voice and gestures, hopes and fears, were so perfectly human that none could mistake them, while he seemed to understand every word of mine. I was troubled at the thought of having to leave him out all night, and of the danger of not finding him in the morning. It seemed impossible to get him to venture. To compel him to try through fear of being abandoned, I started off as if leaving him to his fate, and disappeared back of a hummock, but this did no good; he only lay down and moaned in utter hopeless misery. So, after hiding a few minutes, I went back to the brink of the crevasse, and in a severe tone of voice shouted across to him that now I must certainly leave him, I could. wait no longer, and that, if he would not come, all I could promise was that I would return to seek him next day. I warned him that if he went back to the woods the wolves would kill him, and finished by urging him once more by words and gestures to come on, come on.

He knew very well what I meant, and at last, with the courage of despair, hushed and breathless, he crouched down on the brink in the hollow I had made for my knees, pressed his body against the ice as if trying to get the advantage of the friction of every hair, gazed into the first step, put his little feet together and slid them slowly, slowly over the edge and down into it, bunching all four in it and almost standing on his head. Then, without lifting his feet, as well as I could see through the snow, he slowly worked them over the edge of the step and down into the next and the next in succession in the same way, and gained the end of the bridge. Then, lifting his feet with the regularity and slowness of the vibrations of a seconds pendulum, as if counting and measuring *one-two-three*, holding himself steady against the gusty wind, and giving separate attention to each little step, he gained the foot of the cliff, while I was on my knees leaning over to give him a lift should he succeed in getting within reach of my arm. Here he halted in dead silence, and it was here I feared he might fail, for dogs are poor climbers. I had no cord. If I had had one, I would have dropped a noose over his head and hauled him up. But while I was thinking whether an available cord might be made out of clothing, he was looking keenly into the series of notched steps and finger-holds I had made, as if counting them, and fixing the position of each one of them in his mind. Then suddenly up he came in a springy rush, hooking his paws into the steps and notches so quickly that I could not see how it was done, and whizzed past my head, safe at last!

And now came a scene! "Well done, well done, little boy! Brave boy!" I cried, trying to catch and caress him, but he would not be caught. Never before or since have I seen anything like so passion-ate a revulsion from the depths of despair to exultant, triumphant, uncontrollable joy. He flashed and darted hither and thither as if fairly demented, screaming and shouting, swirling round and round in giddy loops and circles like a leaf in a whirlwind; lying down, and rolling over and over, sidewise and heels over head, and pouring forth a tumultuous flood of hysterical cries and sobs and gasping mutterings. When I ran up to him to shake him, fearing he might die of joy, he flashed off two or three hundred yards, his feet in a mist of motion; then, turning suddenly, came back in a wild rush and launched himself at my face, almost knocking me down, all the time screeching and screaming and shouting as if saying, "Saved! saved! saved!" Then away again, dropping suddenly at times with his feet in the air, trembling and fairly sobbing. Such passionate emotion was enough to kill him. Moses' stately song of triumph after escaping the Egyptians and the Red Sea was nothing to it. Who could have guessed the capacity of the dull, enduring little fellow for all that most stirs this mortal frame? Nobody could have helped crying with him!

But there is nothing like work for toning down excessive fear or joy. So I ran ahead, calling him in as gruff a voice as I could command to come on and stop his nonsense, for we had far to go and it would soon be dark.

Voyage to East Africa

JAN. 16

Fine weather. Left for Victoria Falls about 12:30 p.m. Fine ride along sand flat at base of mountains, gradually rising. At 5:15 at Worsuster. Beautiful town, in long beautiful, level, boulder-strewn glacier valley, in some places several miles wide, perhaps a hundred miles long or more. Finely sculptured mountain range on both sides. Water rather scarce, small streams. Like valleys in S. California. Small vineyards here and there. Grapes ripe. Grain harvested.

At the head of this long mountain-walled valley, our heavy train of a dozen coaches, drawn and pushed by two powerful engines, climbed on wonderful grades (7 or 8%) and curves out upon a vast plateau like those of Arizona in flora bounded by level-topped buttes and peaks. Saw small black monkey walking slowly and indignantly away from the passing train near the head of the pass. Not a cloud in the sky until near sundown when beautiful crimson horizontal plumes decorated the lower sky all around. A most glorious day in every way. The stars shone bright as we sped on over the apparently boundless plain.

JAN. 17

Glorious sunrise. Cloudless. All day on great plateau. Soil red and tawny. Ant nest, dome-shaped, narrow, eighteen inches high. Saw man on horseback driving a flock of ostriches. A remarkable sight to me. Crossed only one river by a fine steel bridge. The Orange River, I suppose. Arrived at Kimberly about 7:20 p.m. Marvelous city, of enormous gray dumps of material hoisted from the

diamond beds. Left Kimberly and the diamond pits at 8:30 p.m.
Dry desert, seemingly endless.

JAN. 18
Wonderful change. All the broad plain or plateau green and even
flowery here and there, and dotted with bushes and small trees.
Mimosa, etc. Some of them in flower. Gradually increasing in size
and number until they darkened the landscape in the distance like
forests. Only a few rounding hills or low mountains visible in the
vast expanse. At 10:00 a.m. ran suddenly into a region of rounded
glaciated hills of metamorphic slate out of which we emerged in
about an hour to a wide plain, green and flowery with dark forested
mountains in the distance. Ground near the track densely covered
with bushes, mostly with yellow-green foliage. Here the first trees
were found, twenty to thirty feet high, eighteen inches in diameter, with lavish undergrowth of bushes. This plain, with its low
forest, extends with great regularity for one hundred and fifty
miles or more. The train had been running through it at twenty
miles speed over six and a half hours, and now, at sundown, there
is no sign of reaching the limit of this strange forest and plain, a
smooth sandstone plain, apparently boundless. Only a small group
of peaks to the westward, seen about 6:00 p.m. A red sandstone in
rounded moutonnée masses and ridgy pavements show here and
there through the almost continuous tufted sod of grasses like
Buffalo grass.

JAN. 19
Cloudy and cool. Magnificent sunrise. Huge compound wing-
shaped masses of clouds, changing to deep velvety maroon and
magenta. A truly glorious spectacle. The same nearly level plateau.
Green, lightly forested, stretching on and on with no boundary in
sight save the sky. No mountains visible. A sea of verdure. Arrived
Bulwayo about 7:00 a.m. Scrawny breakfast at station. Walked
through the town. Forest becoming more varied. Tall palms common, and the low, pale green dwarf species. The ground hillocky.

JAN. 20

Arrive at Victoria Falls station at 7:00 a.m. and have enjoyed a wonderful day, wonderful in many ways; one of the greatest of the great tree days of my lucky life. Inquiring at the hotel if there were any baobabs in the neighborhood, the manager said that he had never heard of a baobab. I explained that it was a large tree, one of the largest of the great trees of the world, and that I had heard that some of them grew at no great distance from here.

After many anxious inquiries I found a bright Negro boy guide who led me direct to the long-dreamed-of African *Adansonia digitata*. I found a large number at a distance of only about a mile or a mile and a half from the head of the Falls, and not over half a mile back from the bank of the river. I discovered specimens showing their different forms, varying from twelve to twenty-four feet in diameter. Most of them about seventy-five to ninety feet high and very wide-spreading, the main branches large, often four to six feet in diameter, gradually dividing into comparatively slender branchlets; many of them drooping, and well-clad with rather pale green five to seven or even nine-fingered leaves. I found a few of the fruits that had fallen on the ground and also some of the wilted flowers. The flowers are white, circular, and about six inches in diameter. This grand tree was first discovered by Michael Adanson of the West Coast near Sierra Leone. It also extends considerably to the north at the head of the Senegal River. I afterwards found it in great abundance at Mozambique, Zanzibar, Desersalaan, Panga, and Mombasa on the East Coast. A red-flowered species *A. madagascariensis* is found on the island of that name. A third species has been found in Australia, *A. gregorii*. It is often called monkey-bread tree. Also cream of tartar tree, from the pleasantly acid juice of the fruit furnishing a refreshing drink. This wonderful tree belongs to the malvaceae. The timber is so soft and spongy that it has no merchantable use, though I was informed that large rain-water tanks were sometimes dug in the broad body of the living tree. It grows scattered here and there among other trees in the general forest, and is easily recognized by its remarkably smooth skin-like bark, and its massive trunk and branches. Altogether I measured and sketched about a dozen specimens. The fruit is green, about six inches long and three in diameter, hanging straight down, and very conspicuous. The leaves are thin, delicate, and smooth. About three to four or five inches long and wide. The bark is gray in color, wonderfully smooth, shining, wrinkled here and there, and slightly corrugated horizontally, but with no furrow like the bark of most other trees. It looks like leather, or the skin of the hippopotamus. On my return trip I noticed a good many in the woods from the car window seventy miles or more to the southward of the falls. On the return trip to Bulwayo I enjoyed the company of Captain Murray, who has charge of the mounted police through a large part of Rhodesia north and south from the Victoria Falls. He kindly promised to send me photographs of the most telling of the Rhodesian trees. Took me to his headquarters at Bulwayo and arranged for my journey to Beira.

JAN. 21
Arrived Bulwayo at 7:00 this morning, having left the Falls at 12:20 p.m. yesterday. Enjoyed view of part of the forest that I had passed through at night on my way North. The baobab is the most interesting feature of the forest for seventy miles south of Victoria Falls. Went to Grand Hotel, Bulwayo. The town is spread over a large level area. The buildings sparsely sprinkled. Will take long to form continuous streets. At hotel all day, resting after wild baobab and Zambesi joy. Strange tree. In bark like skin of elephant. Corrugated and wrinkled like skin of hippopotamus. Very smooth and glossy. Gray, whitish some places. Beautiful five to seven-parted leaves. Huge limbs but well clothed with leaves. So striking in size and form it is easily recognized at a distance of several miles.

The Falls too are grand and novel, and are already drawing large numbers of tourists from all parts of the world. Smoke-like spray is ever ascending, watering the woods in the neighborhood with constant drizzling showers. Large area near the Falls called the "Rainy Woods."

Among the other notable trees of the baobab forest is the Mopani, a fine, large leguminous tree with hard, valuable wood. The Maruba, another large tree, the fruit of which is edible. *Erythima tomentosa*, something like the baobab at a distance, also leguminous. Kigelia has fruit shaped like sausage two feet in length. This large tree is also seen at Victoria Falls. Common in equatorial Africa. It has a sturdy trunk with rough furrowed bark like an oak. Purple tulip-like blossoms. Also three species of palms.

FEB. 7
Start at noon for Antebbe, Uganda. Heavy rain in the morning. Baobabs common along the railroad for twenty or thirty miles, but smaller as the coast is left, though the soil is good. Why is this? Hills grassy, trees and shrubs scattered, fire-scourged. Glacier features. Mountains blue in the distance. Had good fortune as usual in finding two pleasant traveling companions, one a Swiss, who kindly shared his fine luncheon with me, as there is no dining car on the train. At night he gave me one of his rugs as there was no bedding on the train. This friend is a professional hunter with headquarters at Nairobi. The other is Arch-Deacon Binns. Two others joined us in our compartment in the middle of the night. Scotch. One who had often been in Dunbar and knew my friends there. Heard him pronounce "John" and knew him for a Scotchman in the dark, though I was half asleep.

FEB. 8
Country more and more distinctly glacial. See hundreds or thousands of hartbeests and other antelopes, some within stone's throw of the track. Large number of wild ostriches. Grassy plains. No trees or shrubs for miles and miles. Great hills and mountains in the distance. Lovely country. Glacial drift common. Arrived Nairobi at 11:15 a.m. Went to Norfolk Hotel.

FEB. 9
At Hotel. Fine scenery. Heavy rain. Great need of increased hotel accommodations. In rare weather conditions Kaillimanjara visible

one hundred and fifty miles distant from here. Rained for three days on most of way from Mombasa. Rainy season usually begins in March in this part of British East Africa.

FEB. 10

Left Nairobi for Port Florence at noon. Rainy until after dark. Never saw rain so early in the season in the last fourteen years, though only about a month earlier than usual. Railroad runs through beautiful mountain scenery, patches of forest with open grassy prairies, filled-up lake basins. Views of large main valley, very broad, fine in its main lines. Tawny in color from dry grass. Juniper common. Used for lumber, but splits too freely for some purposes, and as usual all the older trees are eaten with dry rot in the center. This is true of all the many species of juniper. Grand views of the great valley. Was kindly given a blanket and pillow by Mr. Rees, the night being very cold, although almost directly on the equator. The elevation at the highest point the railroad passed over during the night was about 8,000 feet above sea level.

FEB. 11

Arrived at Port Florence about 7:00 a.m. Went aboard the good little steamer *Clement Hill* and started for Antebbe at 10:00 a.m. Wonderful picturesque scenery. Low, green, half-forested hills with mountains in the distance. Not very high. Some perhaps about 6,000 feet above the sea. The Victoria Nyanza one of the largest in the world. Second in size only to Lake Superior. Hippopotamus common around the muddy and reedy shores. The lake is comparatively shallow, only about 240 feet at the deepest part. Anchored at dark.

FEB. 12

Started at daybreak. Arrived at Antebbe about 11:00 a.m. at head of a beautiful bay. Measured one tree about six feet in diameter a little way back from the shore. Many are three or four feet, with fine, wide-spreading head. One tree, of moderate size, had noble digitate leaves, fourteen or more, eighteen inches wide. Petioles two feet long. Mr. Rees took me to the Uganda Protectorate.

Spathodia nilotica, has very large flowers.

Canarium schweinfurthii, very large tree.
Thevetia nerriforia, red.
Bauhinia triandra, double leaf.
Randia dummetorium.
Solianum macaranthum.
Maesopsis berchemoides.
Pipledenia africana.
Monodora myristica.

Mr. Rees took me to the Botanical Gardens. Saw the Manager, who kindly ordered his head gardener to show me over the garden and give me specimens of all I wished. A bright, scholarly fellow, Singalese, from Ceylon. There is a species of mourning dove hereabouts which says "Too hot for anything." A lovely creeper going up straight on smooth-barked tree in regular zigzags.

FEB. 13
Started for Kompali at daylight. Arrived about 9:00 a.m. Ride in jinrikisha from port to village, a distance of about seven miles, through beautiful landscape. Extensive and thrifty banana orchards. The fruit red instead of yellow. Interesting swamps full of the famous papyrus growing here naturally. Charming red, blue and white water lilies in the harbor in glorious abundance. Arrived at Kompali in an hour and a half. Returned in one hour. My jinrikisha was hauled and pushed by three lusty Negroes, two pushing and the other in the shafts. Chanted all the way while trotting, the leader rapidly improvising a line, and the chorus sounded like "Harry *Trunk!* Harry *Trunk!*" The leader would say: "The white man is going to see our pretty town." "Harry Trunk. Harry Trunk." "He sees the black man's fine banana field." "Harry Trunk. Harry Trunk." "He is looking at the birds in the trees." "Harry Trunk. Harry Trunk." "The white man's far from his cold, cold home." "Harry Trunk. Harry Trunk." Etc.

FEB. 14
Started for Jinja at 5:00 a.m. Arrived at 11:30 a.m. From the village I went to see the Ripon Falls at the outlet of the great lake, the main

head fountain of the Nile, the distance from the port being only a little over a mile. The fall is only about fifteen or twenty feet over a bar of resisting rock. The fall is divided into three parts and makes a magnificent show of foam. Large numbers of alligators were sunning themselves on the farther bank at the head of the falls, while fishes in large numbers are constantly springing in wide curves in their attempts to ascend the cascade to enter the lake. The broad stream setting out in rapids on its 3,330 mile course is very impressive.

"In 1852 Sir Roderick Murchison advanced the hypothesis that Africa south of the Sahara Desert was a continent of great antiquity, and simplicity, which had maintained the form of a great basin ever since the age of the new red sandstone. He based his theory on the work of Bain, the pioneer of South African geology, summarized in a paper entitled 'On the Antiquity of the Physical Geography of Inner Africa' by R. Murchison, in which he claims that the country is of interest because it was geologically unique in the long conservation of ancient terrestrial conditions."

The famous Ngrurunga (water holes) from J. W. Gregory's book entitled *The Great Rift Valley.*

FEB. 15
Start for Port Florence at 4:00 a.m. Arrived at 5:00 p.m.

FEB. 16
Got aboard the train on the return journey to Mombasa at 7:30 a.m. From the Port a long level valley six to eight miles wide looks like a filled-in part of the Port Florence arm of the lake, extending twenty or thirty miles to the southward, bounded on the west by a range of bold bluffs, separated by wide cirques here and there; and on the east by smooth terraces, extending lakeward parallel to the bluffs. Native villages and fields along the valley. Water lilies at Port Florence, and papyrus. *Kigelia* trees in fruit here and magnificent figs. One near Port Florence, green with dark green foliage, had fruit a half inch in diameter. The trunk about eight feet in diameter, with a dense dome-shaped broad head something like the great banyan of India. Wild mountains after leaving the lake plains,

through which the railroad has been built at great cost. Twenty or thirty steel trestles over gorgeous and fluting ravines in close succession. Some of the passengers saw a lion by the roadside.

FEB. 17

Very cold night. Slept cold, with heavy underclothing, coat and vest, overcoat, and a thick blanket. Elevation of the region about 6,000 to 8,000 feet above the sea. Colder than the Tuolumne Meadows in the spring, though 3,000 feet higher than here. Passed through dense forests about noon, but the greater part of the way is through grassy hills with only detached patches of brush and trees. Extensive wheat fields here and there. Yesterday afternoon and this forenoon near Nivahsa Station and Lake. This remarkable lake is surrounded by a picturesque mountain and hills. Water said to be fresh, though without any visible outlet. Between Nivasha and Nairoba saw Mt. Kilimanjara and Kenia, and many antelopes and zebra, all within short distances of the railroad, and remarkably tame. The latter most at ease as the train rolled past. This afternoon soon after leaving Nairoba saw hundreds or thousands of antelopes, two droves of zebras, and a few ostriches. Some of the antelopes were lying down within a stone's throw of the track, a few of which lay still. Others rose and gazed at the train, and a few ran off to a distance of a quarter of a mile or so. These fine beasts were on a beautiful treeless shrubless plain or prairie. After coming to a plain dotted with small trees and bushes none of the animals were seen. Some parts of the prairie were roughened with moraine boulders, and some places weathered from the bedrock, which occurs here and there in large patches without any kind of soil, something like glacier pavements, with potholes here and there, weathered out by the rain and wind. Some beds of quartz pebbles with large boulders here and there. The stream channels very shallow. All signs point to glaciation no great geological time ago. Most of the animals seen today were on the Athi plain, and have learned that the nearer the railroad the safer they are from the attack of either men or lions. A strip along the track a mile in width had been reserved as a game refuge, which the animals have been quick to discover and flock into it, from all the adjacent region. Saw Kilimanjara again this afternoon. Only its broad base was visible. The head and main body cloud mantled. Saw also many baobabs two hundred and fifty miles or more from Mombasa. One stood near the Makinda Station within six feet or so from the railroad track.

PART FIVE:

The Planet Steward

God's First Temples: How Shall We Preserve Our Forests?

Record-Union:
The forests of coniferous trees growing on our mountain ranges are by far the most destructible of the natural resources of California. Our gold, and silver, and cinnabar are stored in the rocks, locked up in the safest of all banks, so that notwithstanding the world has been making a run upon them for the last twenty-five years, they still pay out steadily and will probably continue to do so centuries hence, like rivers pouring from perennial mountain fountains. The riches of our magnificent soil beds are also comparatively safe, because even the most barbarous methods of wildcat farming cannot effect complete destruction, and however great the impoverishment produced, full restoration of fertility is always possible to the enlightened farmer. But our forest belts are being burned and cut down and wasted like a field of unprotected grain, and once destroyed can never be wholly restored, even by centuries of persistent and painstaking cultivation.

The practical importance of the preservation of our forests is augmented by their relations to climate, soil, and streams. Strip off the woods with their underbrush from the mountain flanks, and the whole state, the lowlands as well as the highlands, would gradually change into a desert. During rainfalls, and when the winter snow was melting, every stream would become a destructive torrent, overflowing its banks, stripping off and carrying away the fertile soils, filling up the lower river channels, and overspreading the lowland fields with detritus to a vastly more destructive degree than all the washings from hydraulic mines concerning which we now hear so much. Dripping forests give rise to moist sheets and currents of air, and the sod of grasses and underbrush thus fostered, together with the roots of trees themselves, absorb and hold back rains and melting snow, yet allowing them to ooze and percolate and flow gently in useful fertilizing streams. Indeed every pine needle and rootlet, as well as fallen trunks and large clasping roots, may be regarded as dams, hoarding the bounty of storm clouds and dispensing it as blessings all through the summer, instead of allowing it to gather and rush headlong in short-lived, devastating floods. Streams taking their rise in deep woods flow unfailingly as those derived from the eternal ice and snow of the Alps. So constant, indeed, and apparent is the relationship between forests and never-failing springs, that effect is frequently mistaken for cause, it being often asserted that line forests will grow only along streamsides where their roots are well watered, when in fact the forests themselves produce many of the streams flowing through them.

The main forest belt of the Sierra is restricted to the western flank, and extends unbrokenly from one end of the range to the other at an elevation of from three to eight thousand feet above sea level. The great master-existence of these noble woods is *Sequoia gigantea*, or big tree. Only two species of sequoia are known to exist in the world. Both belong to California, one being found only in the Sierra, the other (*Sequoia sempervirens*) in the Coast Ranges, although no less than five distinct fossil species have been discovered in the tertiary and cretaceous rocks of Greenland. I would like to call attention to this noble tree, with special reference to its preservation. The species extends from the well known Calaveras groves on the north, to the head of Deer Creek on the south, near the big bend of the Kern River, a distance of about two hundred miles, at an elevation above sea level of from about five to eight thousand feet. From the Calaveras to the south fork of King's River, it occurs only in small isolated groves, and so sparsely and irregularly distributed that two gaps occur nearly forty miles in width, the one between the Calaveras and Tuolumne groves, the other between those of the Fresno and King's rivers. From King's River the belt extends across the broad, rugged basins of the Kaweah and Tule rivers to its southern boundary on Deer Creek, interrupted only by deep, rocky canyons, the width of this portion of the belt being from three to ten miles.

In the northern groves few young trees or saplings are found ready to take the places of the failing old ones, and because these ancient, childless sequoias are the only ones known to botanists, the species has been generally regarded as doomed to speedy extinction, as being nothing more than an expiring remnant of an ancient flora, and that therefore there is no use trying to save it or to prolong its few dying days. This, however, is in the main a mistaken notion, for the Sierra as it now exists never had an ancient flora. All the species now growing on the range have been planted since the close of the glacial period, and the Big Tree has never formed a greater part of these postglacial forests than it does today, however widely it may have been distributed throughout preglacial forests.

In tracing the belt southward, all the phenomena bearing upon its history goes to show that the dominion of *Sequoia gigantea,* as king of California trees, is not yet passing away. No tree in the woods seems more firmly established, or more safely settled in accordance with climate and soil. They fill the woods and form the principal tree, growing heartily on solid ledges, along water courses, in the deep, moist soil of meadows, and upon avalanche and glacial debris, with a multitude of thrifty seedlings and saplings crowding around the aged, ready to take their places and rule the woods.

Nevertheless, Nature in her grandly deliberate way keeps up a rotation of forest crops. Species develop and die like individuals, animal as well as plant. Man himself will as surely become extinct as sequoia or mastodon, and be at length known only as a fossil. Changes of this kind are, however, exceedingly slow in their movements, and, as far as the lives of individuals are concerned, such changes have no appreciable effect. Sequoia seems scarcely further past prime as a species than its companion firs (*Picea amabilis* and *P. grandis*), and judging from its present condition and its ancient history, as far as I have been able to decipher it, our sequoia will live and flourish gloriously until A.D. 15,000 at least—probably for longer—that is, if it be allowed to remain in the hands of nature.

But waste and pure destruction are already taking place at a terrible rate, and unless protective measures be speedily invented and enforced, in a few years this noblest tree-species in the world will present only a few hacked and scarred remnants. The great enemies of forests are fire and the ax. The destructive effects of these, as compared with those caused by the operations of nature, are instantaneous. Floods undermine and kill many a tree, storm winds bend and break, landslips and avalanches overwhelm whole groves, lightning shatters and burns, but the combined effects of all these amount only to a wholesome beauty-producing culture. Last summer I found some five sawmills located in or near the lower edge of the sequoia belt, all of which saw more or less of the big tree into lumber. One of these (Hyde's), situated on the north fork of the Kaweah, cut no less than two million feet of sequoia lumber last season. Most of the Fresno big trees are doomed to feed the mills recently erected near them, and a company has been formed by Chas. Converse to cut the noble forest on the south fork of King's River. In these milling operations, waste far exceeds use. After the choice young manageable trees have been felled, the woods are cleared of limbs and refuse by burning, and in these clearing fires, made with reference to further operations, all the young seedlings and saplings are destroyed, together with many valuable fallen trees and old trees, too large to be cut, thus effectually cutting off all hopes of a renewal of the forest.

These ravages, however, of mill-fires and mill-axes are small as compared with those of the "sheep men's" fires. Incredible numbers of sheep are driven to the mountain pastures every summer, and in order to make easy paths and to improve the pastures, running fires are set everywhere to burn off the old logs and underbrush. These fires are far more universal and destructive than would be guessed. They sweep through nearly the entire forest belt of the range from one extremity to the other, and in the dry weather, before the coming on of winter storms, are very destructive to all kinds of young trees, and especially to sequoia, whose loose, fibrous bark catches and burns at once. Excepting the Calaveras, I, last summer, examined every sequoia grove in the range, together with the main belt extending across the basins of Kaweah and Tule, and found everywhere the most deplorable waste from this cause. Indians burn off underbrush to facilitate deer hunting. Campers of all kinds often permit fires to run, so also do mill-men, but the fires of sheep men probably form more than 90 percent of all destructive fires that sweep the woods.

Fire, then, is the arch destroyer of our forests, and sequoia forests suffer most of all. The young trees are most easily fire killed; the old are most easily burned, and the prostrate trunks, which never rot and would remain valuable until our tenth centennial, are reduced to ashes.

In European countries, especially in France, Germany, Italy, and Austria, the economies of forestry have been carefully studied under the auspices of government, with the most beneficial results. Whether our loose-jointed government is really able or willing to do anything in the matter remains to be seen. If our lawmakers were to discover and enforce any method tending to lessen even in a small degree the destruction going on, they would thus cover a multitude of legislative sins in the eyes of every tree lover. I am satisfied, however, that the question can be intelligently discussed only after a careful survey of our forests has been made, together with studies of the forces now acting upon them.

A law was constructed some years ago making the cutting down of sequoias over sixteen feet in diameter illegal. A more absurd and shortsighted piece of legislation could not be conceived. All the young trees might be cut and burned, and all the old ones might be burned but not cut.

Sacramento Daily Union
February 5, 1876

The Wild Parks and Forest Reservations of the West

Keep not standing fix'd and rooted,
  Briskly venture, briskly roam;
Head and hand, where'er thou foot it,
  And stout heart are still at home.
In each land the sun does visit
  We are gay, whate'er betide:
To give room for wandering is it
  That the world was made so wide.

The tendency nowadays to wander in wildernesses is delightful to see. Thousands of tired, nerve-shaken, over-civilized people are beginning to find out that going to the mountains is going home; that wildness is a necessity; and that mountain parks and reservations are useful not only as fountains of timber and irrigating rivers, but as fountains of life. Awakening from the stupefying effects of the vice of over-industry and the deadly apathy of luxury, they are trying as best they can to mix and enrich their own little ongoings with those of nature, and to get rid of rust and disease. Briskly venturing and roaming, some are washing off sins and cobweb cares of the devil's spinning in all-day storms on mountains; sauntering in rosiny pine woods or in gentian meadows, brushing through chaparral, bending down and parting sweet, flowery sprays; tracing rivers to their sources, getting in touch with the nerves of Mother Earth; jumping from rock to rock, feeling the life of them, learning the songs of them, panting in whole-souled exercise, and rejoicing in deep, long-drawn breaths of pure wildness. This is fine and natural and full of promise. So also is the growing interest in the care and preservation of forests and wild places in general, and in the half-wild parks and gardens of towns. Even the scenery habit in its most artificial forms, mixed with spectacles, silliness, and kodaks; its devotees arrayed more gorgeously than scarlet tanagers, frightening the wild game with red umbrellas—even this is encouraging, and may well be regarded as a hopeful sign of the times.

All the western mountains are still rich in wildness, and by means of good roads are being brought nearer civilization every year. To the sane and free it will hardly seem necessary to cross the continent in search of wild beauty, however easy the way, for they find it in abundance wherever they chance to be. Like Thoreau they see forests in orchards and patches of huckleberry brush, and oceans in ponds and drops of dew. Few in these hot, dim, strenuous times are quite sane or free; choked with care like clocks full of dust, laboriously doing so much good and making so much money—or so little—they are no longer good for themselves.

When, like a merchant taking a list of his goods, we take stock of our wildness, we are glad to see how much of even the most destructible kind is still unspoiled. Looking at our continent as scenery when it was all wild, lying between beautiful seas, the starry sky above it, the starry rocks beneath it, to compare its sides, the East and the West, would be like comparing the sides of a rainbow. But it is no longer equally beautiful. The rainbows of today are, I suppose, as bright as those that first spanned the sky; and some of our landscapes are growing more beautiful from year to year, notwithstanding the clearing, trampling work of civilization. New plants and animals are enriching woods and gardens, and many landscapes wholly new, with divine sculpture and architecture, are just now coming to the light of day as the mantling folds of creative glaciers are being withdrawn, and life in a thousand cheerful, beautiful forms is pushing into them, and newborn rivers are beginning to sing and shine in them. The old rivers, too, are growing longer, like healthy trees, gaining new branches and lakes as the residual glaciers at their highest sources on the mountains recede, while the root-like branches in their flat deltas are at the same time spreading farther and wider into the seas and making new lands.

Under the control of the vast mysterious forces of the interior of the earth, all the continents and islands are slowly rising or sinking. Most of the mountains are diminishing in size under the wearing action of the weather, though a few are increasing in height and girth, especially the volcanic ones, as fresh floods of molten rocks are piled on their summits and spread in successive layers, like the wood-rings of trees, on their sides. New mountains, also, are being created from time to time as islands in lakes and seas, or as subordinate cones on the slopes of old ones, thus in some measure balancing the waste of old beauty with new. Man, too, is making many far-reaching changes. This most influential half animal, half angel is rapidly multiplying and spreading, covering the seas and lakes with ships, the land with huts, hotels, cathedrals, and clustered city shops and homes, so that soon, it would seem, we may have to go farther than Nansen to find a good sound solitude. None of nature's landscapes are ugly so long as they are wild; and much, we can say comfortingly, must always be in great part wild, particularly the sea and the sky, the floods of light from the stars, and the warm, unspoilable heart of the earth, infinitely beautiful, though only dimly visible to the eye of imagination. The geysers, too, spouting from the hot underworld; the steady, long-lasting glaciers on the mountains, obedient only to the sun; Yosemite domes and the tremendous grandeur of rocky canyons and mountains in general—these must always be wild, for man can change them and mar them hardly more than can the butterflies that hover above them. But the continent's outer beauty is fast passing away, especially the plant part of it, the most destructible and most universally charming of all.

Only thirty years ago, the great Central Valley of California, five hundred miles long and fifty miles wide, was one bed of golden and purple flowers. Now it is ploughed and pastured out of existence, gone forever—scarce a memory of it left in fence corners and along the bluffs of the streams. The gardens of the Sierra, also, and the noble forests in both the reserved and unreserved portions are sadly hacked and trampled, notwithstanding the ruggedness of the topography—all excepting those of the parks guarded by a few soldiers. In the noblest forests of the world, the ground, once divinely beautiful, is desolate and repulsive, like a face ravaged by disease. This is true also of many other Pacific Coast and Rocky Mountain valleys and forests. The same fate, sooner or later, is awaiting them all, unless awakening public opinion comes forward to stop it. Even the great deserts in Arizona, Nevada, Utah, and New Mexico, which offer so little to attract settlers, and which a few years ago pioneers were afraid of, as places of desolation and death, are now taken as pastures at the rate of one or two square miles per cow, and of course their plant treasures are passing away—the delicate *Abronias, Phloxes, Gilias,* etc. Only a few of the bitter, thorny, unbitable shrubs are left, and the sturdy cacti that defend themselves with bayonets and spears.

Most of the wild plant wealth of the East also has vanished— gone into dusty history. Only vestiges of its glorious prairie and woodland wealth remain to bless humanity in boggy, rocky, unploughable places. Fortunately, some of these are purely wild and go far to keep nature's love visible. White water lilies, with rootstocks deep and safe in mud, still send up every summer a Milky Way of starry, fragrant flowers around a thousand lakes, and many a tuft of wild grass waves its panicles on mossy rocks, beyond reach of trampling feet, in company with saxifrages, bluebells, and ferns. Even in the midst of farmers' fields, precious *Sphagnum* bogs, too soft for the feet of cattle, are preserved with their charming plants unchanged—*Chiogenes, Andromeda, Kalmia, Linnaea, Arethusa,* etc. *Calypso borealis* still hides in the arbor vitae swamps of Canada, and away to the southward there are a few unspoiled swamps, big ones, where miasma, snakes, and alligators, like guardian angels, defend their treasures and keep them as pure as paradise. And beside a' that and a' that, the East is blessed with good winters and blossoming clouds that shed white flowers over all the land, covering every scar and making the saddest landscape divine at least once a year.

The most extensive, least spoiled, and most unspoilable of the gardens of the continent are the vast tundras of Alaska. In summer they extend smooth, even, undulating, continuous beds of flowers and leaves from about latitude 62 to the shores of the Arctic Ocean; and in winter sheets of snow flowers make all the country shine, one mass of white radiance like a star. Nor are these Arctic plant people the pitiful frost-pinched unfortunates they are guessed to be by those who have never seen them. Though lowly in stature, keeping near the frozen ground as if loving it, they are bright and cheery, and speak nature's love as plainly as their big relatives of the South. Tenderly happed and tucked in beneath downy snow to sleep through the long, white winter, they make haste to bloom in the spring without trying to grow tall, though some rise high enough to ripple and wave in the wind, and display masses of color—yellow, purple, and blue—so rich that they look like beds of rainbows, and are visible miles and miles away.

As early as June one may find the showy *Geum glaciale* in flower, and the dwarf willows putting forth myriad fuzzy catkins, to be followed quickly, especially on the dryer ground, by *Mertensia, Eritrichium, Polemonium, Oxytropis, Astragalus, Lathyrus, Lupinus, Myosotis, Dodecatheon, Arnica, Chrysanthemum, Nardosmia, Saussurea, Senecio, Erigeron, Matrecaria, Caltha, Valeriana, Stellaria, Tofieldia, Polygonum, Papaver, Phlox, Lychnis, Cheiranthus, Linnaea,* and a host of *Drabas, Saxifrages,* and heathworts, with bright stars and bells in glorious profusion, particularly *Cassiope, Andromeda, Ledum, Pyrola,* and *Vaccinium—Cassiope* the most abundant and beautiful of them all. Many grasses also grow here, and wave fine purple spikes and panicles over the other flowers—*Poa, Aira, Calamagrostis, Alopecurus, Trisetum, Elymus, Festuca, Glyceria,* etc. Even ferns are found thus far north, carefully and comfortably unrolling their precious fronds—*Aspidium, Cystopteris,* and *Woodsia,* all growing on a sumptuous bed of mosses and lichens; not the scaly lichens seen on rails and trees and fallen logs to the southward, but massive, round-headed, finely colored plants like corals, wonderfully beautiful, worth going round the world to see. I should like to mention all the plant friends I found in a summer's wanderings in this cool reserve, but I fear few would care to read their names, although everybody, I am sure, would love them could they see them blooming and rejoicing at home.

On my last visit to the region about Kotzebue Sound, near the middle of September 1881, the weather was so fine and mellow

that it suggested the Indian summer of the eastern states. The
winds were hushed, the tundra glowed in creamy golden sunshine, and the colors of the ripe foliage of the heathworts, willows,
and birch—red, purple, and yellow, in pure bright tones—were
enriched with those of berries which were scattered everywhere,
as if they had been showered from the clouds like hail. When
I was back a mile or two from the shore, reveling in this color-
glory, and thinking how fine it would be could I cut a square of
the tundra sod of conventional picture size, frame it, and hang it
among the paintings on my study walls at home, saying to myself,
"Such a nature painting taken at random from any part of the
thousand-mile bog would make the other pictures look dim and
coarse," I heard merry shouting, and, looking round, saw a band
of Eskimos—men, women, and children, loose and hairy like wild
animals—running toward me. I could not guess at first what they
were seeking, for they seldom leave the shore; but soon they told
me, as they threw themselves down, sprawling and laughing, on
the mellow bog, and began to feast on the berries. A lively picture
they made, and a pleasant one, as they frightened the whirring
ptarmigans, and surprised their oily stomachs with the beautiful
acid berries of many kinds, and filled sealskin bags with them to
carry away for festive days in winter.

Nowhere else on my travels have I seen so much warm-blooded,
rejoicing life as in this grand Arctic reservation, by so many regarded
as desolate. Not only are there whales in abundance along the
shores, and innumerable seals, walruses, and white bears, but on
the tundras, great herds of fat reindeer and wild sheep, foxes, hares,
mice, piping marmots, and birds. Perhaps more birds are born
here than in any other region of equal extent on the continent. Not
only do strong-winged hawks, eagles, and waterfowl, to whom the
length of the continent is merely a pleasant excursion, come up here
every summer in great numbers, but also many short-winged war-
blers, thrushes, and finches, repairing hither to rear their young in
safety, reinforce the plant bloom with their plumage, and sweeten
the wilderness with song; flying all the way, some of them, from
Florida, Mexico, and Central America. In coming north they are

coming home, for they were born here, and they go south only to spend the winter months, as New Englanders go to Florida. Sweet-voiced troubadours, they sing in orange groves and vine-clad magnolia woods in winter, in thickets of dwarf birch and alder in summer, and sing and chatter more or less all the way back and forth, keeping the whole country glad. Oftentimes, in New England, just as the last snow patches are melting and the sap in the maples begins to flow, the blessed wanderers may be heard about orchards and the edges of fields where they have stopped to glean a scanty meal, not tarrying long, knowing they have far to go. Tracing the footsteps of spring, they arrive in their tundra homes in June or July, and set out on their return journey in September, or as soon as their families are able to fly well.

This is nature's own reservation, and every lover of wildness will rejoice with me that by kindly frost it is so well defended. The discovery lately made that it is sprinkled with gold may cause some alarm; for the strangely exciting stuff makes the timid bold enough for anything, and the lazy destructively industrious. Thousands at least half insane are now pushing their way into it, some by the southern passes over the mountains, perchance the first mountains they have ever seen—sprawling, struggling, gasping for breath, as, laden with awkward, merciless burdens of provisions and tools, they climb over rough-angled boulders and cross thin miry bogs. Some are going by the mountains and rivers to the eastward through Canada, tracing the old romantic ways of the Hudson Bay traders; others by Bering Sea and the Yukon, sailing all the way, getting glimpses perhaps of the famous fur seals, the ice floes, and the innumerable islands and bars of the great Alaska river. In spite of frowning hardships and the frozen ground, the Klondike gold will increase the crusading crowds for years to come, but comparatively little harm will be done. Holes will be burned and dug into the hard ground here and there, and into the quartz-ribbed mountains and hills; ragged towns like beaver and muskrat villages will be built, and mills and locomotives will make rumbling, screeching, disenchanting noises; but the miner's pick will not be followed far by the plough, at least not until nature is ready to unlock the frozen soil

beds with her slow-turning climate key. On the other hand, the
roads of the pioneer miners will lead many a lover of wildness into
the heart of the reserve, who without them would never see it.

In the meantime, the wildest health and pleasure grounds accessible and available to tourists seeking escape from care and dust
and early death are the parks and reservations of the West. There
are four National Parks—the Yellowstone, Yosemite, General
Grant, and Sequoia—all within easy reach, and thirty forest reservations, a magnificent realm of woods, most of which, by rail-
roads and trails and open ridges, is also fairly accessible, not only
to the determined traveler rejoicing in difficulties, but to those
(may their tribe increase) who, not tired, not sick, just naturally
take wing every summer in search of wildness. The forty million
acres of these reserves are in the main unspoiled as yet, though
sadly wasted and threatened on their more open margins by the ax
and fire of the lumberman and prospector, and by hoofed locusts,
which, like the winged ones, devour every leaf within reach, while
the shepherds and owners set fires with the intention of making a
blade of grass grow in the place of every tree, but with the result of
killing both the grass and the trees.

Sources

Part One: The Visionary Inventor

"Knowledge and Inventions" and "The World and the University" from *The Story of My Boyhood and Youth,* Ch. 7 and Ch. 8, from *John Muir: Nature Writings,* William Cronon, ed. (New York: Library of America, 1997), 117–142.

Part Two: The Wandering Minstrel

"Through the Cumberland Mountains," from *A Thousand-Mile Walk to the Gulf* by John Muir (Boston: Houghton Mifflin—Mariner Books, 1916), 30–33, 60–63, 123–142.

Part Three: The Nature Scribe and Rhapsode

"A Near View of the High Sierra," from *The Mountains of California* by John Muir (New York: Modern Library, 2001), 344–360.

"A Windstorm in the Forest," from *The Mountains of California.*

"Yosemite Falls at Midnight," letter from John Muir to Jeanne (Mrs. Ezra S.) Carr, April 3, 1871, from *The Life and Letters of John Muir,* William Frederic Bade, ed. (Boston: Houghton Mifflin, 1924), 1:249–252.

"Nut Time in Squirrelville," letter from John Muir to Jeanne (Mrs. Ezra S.) Carr, dated "Nut Time," ca. 1870, from *The Life and Letters of John Muir,* 1:270–273.

"Yosemite Glaciers," originally published in the *New York Tribune,* Dec. 5, 1871, from *John Muir: Nature Writings,* 577–586.

Part Four: The Global Adventurer

"Eskimos and Walrus," from *The Cruise of the Corwin* by John Muir (San Francisco: Sierra Club, 1993), 48–55.

"Stickeen vs. the Glacier," from *Stickeen* by John Muir (Berkeley: Heyday Books, 1990), 39–64.

"Voyage to East Africa," from *John Muir's Last Journey*, Michael P. Branch, ed. (Washington, D.C.: Island Press, 2001) 107–114.

Part Five: The Planet Steward

"God's First Temples: How Shall We Preserve Our Forests?" originally published in the *Sacramento Daily Union*, Feb. 5, 1876, from *John Muir: Nature Writings*, 629–633.

"The Wild Parks and Forest Reservations of the West," originally published in *Atlantic Monthly*, August 1897, from *Our National Parks* by John Muir (San Francisco: Sierra Club Books, 1991), 1–10.

Major Works by John Muir
(in order of publication)

The Mountains of California (1894)
Our National Parks (1901)
Stickeen (1909)
My First Summer in the Sierra (1911)
The Yosemite (1912)
The Story of My Boyhood and Youth (1913)
Travels in Alaska (1915)
A Thousand-Mile Walk to the Gulf (1916)

About the Editor

Fred D. White, a native Californian, was born in Los Angeles in 1943, in the very same hospital—California Hospital—in which John Muir had died twenty-nine years earlier. White received his Ph.D. in English from the University of Iowa and his B.A. and M.A. in English from the University of Minnesota, where he studied with the distinguished poet-critics Allen Tate and John Berryman. A professor at Santa Clara University since 1980, he teaches writing, including a course in writing about nature and the environment (which he also taught for two summers in Trinidad and Tobago). In 1997 he received the Louis and Dorina Brutocao Award for Teaching Excellence. His other books include *The Daily Writer: 366 Meditations for a Productive and Meaningful Writing Life* (Writer's Digest Books, 2008); *Approaching Emily Dickinson* (Camden House, 2008); *Life Writing* (Quill Driver Books, 2004); *The Well-Crafted Argument,* coauthored with Simone Billings (Houghton Mifflin, 2002, now in its third edition); and *Communicating Technology* (HarperCollins, 1996). His recent essays, fiction, and poetry have appeared in *The Cambridge Companion to Emily Dickinson,* ed. Wendy Martin; *The Chronicle of Higher Education; College Literature; Confrontation; Fantastic Odysseys,* ed. Mary Pharr; *Drexel Online Journal; The Pedestal; Pleiades;* and the *San Jose Mercury News.* He lives in San Mateo, California, with his wife, Therese (an attorney), and their imperious cat, Cordelia.

31901065886840